CW00370100

THE HOME OF A SPIDER

Fresh Fields

Fredonia Books
Amsterdam, The Netherlands

Fresh Fields

by John Burroughs

ISBN 1-58963-054-8

Copyright © 2001 by Fredonia Books

Reprinted from the 1912 edition

Fredonia Books
Amsterdam, The Netherlands
http://www.FredoniaBooks.com

All rights reserved, including the right to reproduce this book, or portions thereof, in any form.

In order to make original editions of historical works available to scholars at an economical price, this facsimile of the original edition of 1912 is reproduced from the best available copy and has been digitally enhanced to improve legibility, but the text remains unaltered to retain historical authenticity.

CONTENTS

FRESH FIELDS

I

NATURE IN ENGLAND

I

THE first whiff we got of transatlantic nature
was the peaty breath of the peasant chimneys
of Ireland while we were yet many miles at sea.
What a homelike, fireside smell it was! it seemed
to make something long forgotten stir within one.
One recognizes it as a characteristic Old World
odor, it savors so of the soil and of a ripe and mellow antiquity. I know no other fuel that yields so
agreeable a perfume as peat. Unless the Irishman
in one has dwindled to a very small fraction, he
will be pretty sure to dilate his nostrils and feel
some dim awakening of memory on catching the
scent of this ancestral fuel. The fat, unctuous
peat, — the pith and marrow of ages of vegetable
growth, — how typical it is of much that lies there
before us in the elder world; of the slow ripenings
and accumulations, of extinct life and forms, decayed
civilizations, of ten thousand growths and achieve-

ments of the hand and soul of man, now reduced
to their last modicum of fertilizing mould!

With the breath of the chimney there came presently the chimney swallow, and dropped much fa-
tigued upon the deck of the steamer. It was a
still more welcome and suggestive token, — the bird
of Virgil and of Theocritus, acquainted with every
cottage roof and chimney in Europe, and with the
ruined abbeys and castle walls. Except its lighter-
colored breast, it seemed identical with our barn
swallow; its little black cap appeared pulled down
over its eyes in the same manner, and its glossy
steel-blue coat, its forked tail, its infantile feet, and
its cheerful twitter were the same. But its habits
are different; for in Europe this swallow builds in
chimneys, and the bird that answers to our chimney
swallow, or swift, builds in crevices in barns and
houses.

We did not suspect we had taken aboard our
pilot in the little swallow, yet so it proved: this
light navigator always hails from the port of bright,
warm skies; and the next morning we found ourselves sailing between shores basking in full summer sunshine. Those who, after ten days of sorrowing and fasting in the desert of the ocean, have
sailed up the Frith of Clyde, and thence up the
Clyde to Glasgow, on the morning of a perfect mid-
May day, the sky all sunshine, the earth all verdure, know what this experience is; and only those
can know it. It takes a good many foul days in
Scotland to breed one fair one: but when the fair

day does come, it is worth the price paid for it. The soul and sentiment of all fair weather is in it; it is the flowering of the meteorological influences, the rose on this thorn of rain and mist. These fair days, I was told, may be quite confidently looked for in May; we were so fortunate as to experience a series of them, and the day we entered port was such a one as you would select from a hundred.

The traveler is in a mood to be pleased after clearing the Atlantic gulf; the eye in its exuberance is full of caresses and flattery, and the deck of a steamer is a rare vantage-ground on any occasion of sight-seeing; it affords just the isolation and elevation needed. Yet fully discounting these favorable conditions, the fact remains that Scotch sunshine is bewitching, and that the scenery of the Clyde is unequaled by any other approach to Europe. It is Europe, abridged and assorted and passed before you in the space of a few hours, — the highlands and lochs and castle-crowned crags on the one hand; and the lowlands, with their parks and farms, their manor halls and matchless verdure, on the other. The eye is conservative, and loves a look of permanence and order, of peace and contentment; and these Scotch shores, with their stone houses, compact masonry, clean fields, grazing herds, ivied walls, massive foliage, perfect roads, verdant mountains, etc., fill all the conditions. We pause an hour in front of Greenock, and then, on the crest of the tide, make our way slowly upward. The landscape closes around us. We can almost

hear the cattle ripping off the lush grass in the
fields. One feels as if he could eat grass himself.
It is pastoral paradise. We can see the daisies and
buttercups; and from above a meadow on the right
a part of the song of a skylark reaches my ear. Indeed, not a little of the charm and novelty of this
part of the voyage was the impression it made as
of going afield in an ocean steamer. We had suddenly passed from a wilderness of waters into a ver-
durous, sunlit landscape, where scarcely any water
was visible. The Clyde, soon after you leave
Greenock, becomes little more than a large, deep
canal, inclosed between meadow banks, and from
the deck of the great steamer only the most charming rural sights and sounds greet you. You are at
sea amid verdant parks and fields of clover and
grain. You behold farm occupations — sowing,
planting, plowing — as from the middle of the
Atlantic. Playful heifers and skipping lambs take
the place of the leaping dolphins and the basking
swordfish. The ship steers her way amid turnip-
fields and broad acres of newly planted potatoes.
You are not surprised that she needs piloting. A
little tug with a rope at her bow pulls her first this
way and then that, while one at her stern nudges
her right flank and then her left. Presently we
come to the ship-building yards of the Clyde, where
rural, pastoral scenes are strangely mingled with
those of quite another sort. "First a cow and then
an iron ship," as one of the voyagers observed.
Here a pasture or a meadow, or a field of wheat or

oats, and close beside it, without an inch of waste or neutral ground between, rise the skeletons of innumerable ships, like a forest of slender growths of iron, with the workmen hammering amid it like so many noisy woodpeckers. It is doubtful if such a scene can be witnessed anywhere else in the world, — an enormous mechanical, commercial, and architectural interest, alternating with the quiet and simplicity of inland farms and home occupations. You could leap from the deck of a half-finished ocean steamer into a field of waving wheat or Winchester beans. These vast shipyards appear to be set down here upon the banks of the Clyde without any interference with the natural surroundings of the place.

Of the factories and foundries that put this iron in shape you get no hint; here the ships rise as if they sprouted from the soil, without waste or litter, but with an incessant din. They stand as thickly as a row of cattle in stanchions, almost touching each other, and in all stages of development. Now and then a stall will be vacant, the ship having just been launched, and others will be standing with flags flying and timbers greased or soaped, ready to take to the water at the word. Two such, both large ocean steamers, waited for us to pass. We looked back, saw the last block or wedge knocked away from one of them, and the monster ship sauntered down to the water and glided out into the current in the most gentle, nonchalant way imaginable. I wondered at her slow pace, and at the grace and composure with which she took to the water; the problem nicely studied and solved, — just power enough, and not an ounce to spare. The vessels are launched diagonally up or down stream, on account of the narrowness of the channel. But to see such a brood of ships, the largest in the world, hatched upon the banks of such a placid little river, amid such quiet country scenes, is a novel experience. But this is Britain, — a little island, with little lakes, little rivers, quiet, bosky fields, but mighty interests and power that reach round the world. I was conscious that the same scene at home would have been less pleasing. It would not have been so compact and tidy. There would not have been a garden of ships and a garden of turnips side by side; haymakers and shipbuilders in adjoining fields; milch-cows and iron steamers seeking the water within sight of each other. We leave wide margins and ragged edges in this country, and both man and nature sprawl about at greater lengths than in the Old World.

For the rest I was perhaps least prepared for the utter tranquillity, and shall I say domesticity, of the mountains. At a distance they appear to be covered with a tender green mould that one could brush away with his hand. On nearer approach it is seen to be grass. They look nearly as rural and pastoral as the fields. Goat Fell is steep and stony, but even it does not have a wild and barren look. At home, one thinks of a mountain as either a vast pile of barren, frowning rocks and precipices, or else a steep acclivity covered with a tangle of primitive forest timber. But here, the mountains are high, grassy sheep-walks, smooth, treeless, rounded, and as green as if dipped in a fountain of perpetual spring. I did not wish my Catskills any different; but I wondered what would need to be done to them to make them look like these Scotch highlands. Cut away their forests, rub down all inequalities in their surfaces, pulverizing their loose bowlders; turf them over, leaving the rock to show through here and there, — then, with a few large black patches to represent the heather, and the softening and ameliorating effect of a mild, humid climate, they might in time come to bear some resemblance to these shepherd mountains. Then over all the landscape is that new look, — that mellow, legendary, half-human expression which nature wears in these ancestral lands, an expression familiar in pictures and in literature, but which a native of our side of the Atlantic has never before seen in gross, material objects and open-air spaces, — the added charm of the sentiment of time and human history, the ripening and ameliorating influence of long ages of close and loving occupation of the soil, — naturally a deep, fertile soil under a mild, very humid climate.

There is an unexpected, an unexplained lure and attraction in the landscape, — a pensive, reminiscent feeling in the air itself. Nature has grown mellow under these humid skies, as in our fiercer climate she grows harsh and severe. One sees at once why this fragrant Old World has so dominated the affections and the imaginations of our artists and poets: it is saturated with human qualities; it is unctuous with the ripeness of ages, the very marrowfat of time.

II

I had come to Great Britain less to see the noted sights and places than to observe the general face of nature. I wanted to steep myself long and well in that mellow, benign landscape, and put to further tests the impressions I had got of it during a hasty visit one autumn, eleven years before. Hence I was mainly intent on roaming about the country, it mattered little where. Like an attic stored with relics and heirlooms, there is no place in England where you cannot instantly turn from nature to scenes and places of deep historical or legendary or artistic interest.

My journal of travel is a brief one, and keeps to a few of the main lines. After spending a couple of days in Glasgow, we went down to Alloway, in Burns's country, and had our first taste of the beauty and sweetness of rural Britain, and of the privacy and comfort of a little Scotch inn. The weather was exceptionally fair, and the mellow Ayrshire landscape, threaded by the Doon, a perpetual delight. Thence we went north on a short tour through the Highlands, — up Loch Lomond, down Loch Katrine, and through the Trosachs to Callander, and thence to Stirling and Edinburgh. After a few days in the Scotch capital we set out for Carlyle's country, where we passed five delightful days. The next week found us in Wordsworth's land, and the 10th of June in London. After a week here I went down into Surrey and Hants, in quest of the nightingale, for four or five days. Till the middle of July I hovered about London, making frequent excursions into the country, — east, south, north, west, and once across the channel into France, where I had a long walk over the hills about Boulogne. July 15 we began our return journey northward, stopping a few days at Stratford, where I found the Red Horse Inn sadly degenerated from excess of travel. Thence again into the Lake region for a longer stay. From Grasmere we went into north Wales, and did the usual touring and sight-seeing around and over the mountains. The last week of July we were again in Glasgow, from which port we sailed on our homeward voyage July 29.

With a suitable companion, I should probably have made many long pedestrian tours. As it was, I took many short but delightful walks both in England and Scotland, with a half day's walk in the north of Ireland about Moville. 'T is an admirable country to walk in, — the roads are so dry and smooth and of such easy grade, the footpaths so numerous and so bold, and the climate so cool and tonic. One night, with a friend, I walked from Rochester to Maidstone, part of the way in a slow rain and part of the way in the darkness. We had proposed to put up at some one of the little

inns on the road, and get a view of the weald of
Kent in the morning; but the inns refused us entertainment, and we were compelled to do the eight
miles at night, stepping off very lively the last four
in order to reach Maidstone before the hotels were
shut up, which takes place at eleven o'clock.   I
learned this night how fragrant the English elder is
while in bloom, and that distance lends enchantment to the smell.   When I plucked the flowers,
which seemed precisely like our own, the odor was
rank and disagreeable; but at the distance of a few
yards it floated upon the moist air, a spicy and
pleasing perfume.   The elder here grows to be a
veritable tree; I saw specimens seven or eight
inches in diameter and twenty feet high.   In the
morning we walked back by a different route, taking in Boxley Church, where the pilgrims used to
pause on their way to Canterbury, and getting many
good views of Kent grain-fields and hop-yards.
Sometimes the road wound through the landscape
like a footpath, with nothing between it and the
rank-growing crops.   An occasional newly-plowed
field presented a curious appearance.   The soil is
upon the chalk formation, and is full of large fragments of flint.   These work out upon the surface,
and, being white and full of articulations and processes, give to the ground the appearance of being
thickly strewn with bones, — with thigh bones
greatly foreshortened.   Yet these old bones in skill-
ful hands make a most effective building material.
They appear in all the old churches and ancient

buildings in the south of England. Broken squarely off, the flint shows a fine semi-transparent surface that, in combination with coarser material, has a remarkable crystalline effect. One of the most delicious bits of architectural decoration I saw in England was produced, in the front wall of one of the old buildings attached to the cathedral at Canterbury, by little squares of these flints in brick panel-work. The cool, pellucid, illuminating effect of the flint was just the proper foil to the warm, glowing, livid brick.

From Rochester we walked to Gravesend, over Gad's Hill; the day soft and warm, half sunshine, half shadow; the air full of the songs of skylarks; a rich, fertile landscape all about us; the waving wheat just in bloom, dashed with scarlet poppies; and presently, on the right, the Thames in view dotted with vessels. Seldom any cattle or grazing herds in Kent; the ground is too valuable; it is all given up to wheat, oats, barley, hops, fruit, and various garden produce.

A few days later we walked from Feversham to Canterbury, and from the top of Harbledown hill saw the magnificent cathedral suddenly break upon us as it did upon the footsore and worshipful pilgrims centuries ago. At this point, it is said, they knelt down, which seems quite probable, the view is so imposing. The cathedral stands out from and above the city, as if the latter were the foundation upon which it rested. On this walk we passed several of the famous cherry orchards of Kent, the

thriftiest trees and the finest fruit I ever saw. We
invaded one of the orchards, and proposed to pur-
chase some of the fruit of the men engaged in gathering it.   But they refused to sell it; had no right
to do so, they said; but one of them followed us
across the orchard, and said in a confidential way
that he would see that we had some cherries.   He
filled my companion's hat, and accepted our shilling
with alacrity.   In getting back into the highway,
over the wire fence, I got my clothes well tarred
before I was aware of it.   The fence proved to be
well besmeared with a mixture of tar and grease, —
an ingenious device for marking trespassers.   We
sat in the shade of a tree and ate our fruit and
scraped our clothes, while a troop of bicyclists filed
by.   About the best glimpses I had of Canterbury
cathedral — after the first view from Harbledown
hill — were obtained while lying upon my back on
the grass, under the shadow of its walls, and gazing
up at the jackdaws flying about the central tower
and going out and in weather-worn openings three
hundred feet above me.   There seemed to be some
wild, pinnacled mountain peak or rocky ledge up
there toward the sky, where the fowls of the air
had made their nests, secure from molestation.
The way the birds make themselves at home about
these vast architectural piles is very pleasing.
Doves, starlings, jackdaws, swallows, sparrows, take
to them as to a wood or to a cliff.   If there were
only something to give a corresponding touch of
nature or a throb of life inside!   But their interiors

are only impressive sepulchres, tombs within a
tomb. Your own footfalls seem like the echo of
past ages. These cathedrals belong to the pleisto-
cene period of man's religious history, the period
of gigantic forms. How vast, how monstrous, how
terrible in beauty and power! but in our day as
empty and dead as the shells upon the shore. The
cold, thin ecclesiasticism that now masquerades in
them hardly disturbs the dust in their central aisles.
I saw five worshipers at the choral service in Canterbury, and about the same number of curious
spectators. For my part, I could not take my eyes
off the remnants of some of the old stained windows
up aloft. If I worshiped at all, it was my devout
admiration of those superb relics. There could be
no doubt about the faith that inspired those. Below them were some gorgeous modern memorial
windows: stained glass, indeed! loud, garish, thin,
painty; while these were like a combination of precious stones and gems, full of depth and richness of
tone, and, above all, serious, not courting your
attention. My eye was not much taken with them
at first, and not till after it had recoiled from the
hard, thin glare in my immediate front.

From Canterbury I went to Dover, and spent
part of a day walking along the cliffs to Folkestone.
There is a good footpath that skirts the edge of the
cliffs, and it is much frequented. It is characteristic of the compactness and neatness of this little
island, that there is not an inch of waste land along
this sea margin; the fertile rolling landscape, wav-

ing with wheat and barley, and with grass just ready for the scythe, is cut squarely off by the sea; the plow and the reaper come to the very brink of the chalky cliffs. As you sit down on Shakespeare's Cliff, with your feet dangling in the air at a height of three hundred and fifty feet, you can reach back and pluck the grain heads and the scarlet poppies. Never have I seen such quiet pastoral beauty take such a sudden leap into space. Yet the scene is tame in one sense: there is no hint of the wild and the savage; the rock is soft and friable, a kind of chalky bread, which the sea devours readily; the hills are like freshly cut loaves; slice after slice has been eaten away by the hungry elements. Sitting here, I saw no "crows and choughs" winging "the midway air," but a species of hawk, "haggards of the rocks," were disturbed in the niches beneath me, and flew along from point to point.

> "The murmuring surge,
> That on the unnumber'd idle pebbles chafes,
> Cannot be heard so high."

I had wondered why Shakespeare had made his seashores pebbly instead of sandy, and now I saw why: they are pebbly, with not a grain of sand to be found. This chalk formation, as I have already said, is full of flint nodules; and as the shore is eaten away by the sea, these rounded masses remain. They soon become worn into smooth pebbles, which beneath the pounding of the surf give out a strange clinking, rattling sound. Across the Channel, on the French side, there is more sand, but it is of the hue of mud and not pleasing to look upon.

Of other walks I had in England, I recall with pleasure a Sunday up the Thames toward Windsor: the day perfect, the river alive with row-boats, the shore swarming with pedestrians and picnickers; young athletic London, male and female, rushing forth as hungry for the open air and the water as young mountain herds for salt. I never saw or imagined anything like it. One shore of the Thames, sometimes the right, sometimes the left, it seems, belongs to the public. No private grounds, however lordly, are allowed to monopolize both sides.

Another walk was about Winchester and Salisbury, with more cathedral-viewing. One of the most human things to be seen in the great cathedrals is the carven image of some old knight or warrior prince resting above his tomb, with his feet upon his faithful dog. I was touched by this remembrance of the dog. In all cases he looked alert and watchful, as if guarding his master while he slept. I noticed that Cromwell's soldiers were less apt to batter off the nose and ears of the dog than they were those of the knight.

At Stratford I did more walking. After a row on the river, we strolled through the low, grassy field in front of the church, redolent of cattle and clover, and sat for an hour on the margin of the stream and enjoyed the pastoral beauty and the sunshine. In the afternoon (it was Sunday) I

walked across the fields to Shottery, and then followed the road as it wound amid the quaint little
thatched cottages till it ended at a stile from which
a footpath led across broad, sunny fields to a stately
highway.   To give a more minute account of English country scenes and sounds in midsummer, I
will here copy some jottings in my note-book, made
then and there: —

"*July* 16.   In the fields beyond Shottery.
Bright and breezy, with appearance of slight showers in the distance.   Thermometer probably about
seventy; a good working temperature.   Clover —
white, red, and yellow (white predominating) — in
the fields all about me.   The red very ruddy; the
white large.   The only noticeable bird voice that
of the yellow-hammer, two or three being within
ear-shot.   The song is much like certain sparrow
songs, only inferior: *Sip, sip, sip, see-e-e-e;* or,
If, if, if you ple-e-ease.   Honey-bees on the
white clover.   Turf very thick and springy, sup
porting two or three kinds of grass resembling red
top and bearded rye-grass.   Narrow-leaved plantain,
a few buttercups, a small yellow flower unknown to
me (probably ladies' fingers), also a species of dandelion and prunella.   The land thrown into marked
swells twenty feet broad.   Two Sunday-school girls
lying on the grass in the other end of the field.   A
number of young men playing some game, perhaps
cards, seated on the ground in an adjoining field.
Scarcely any signs of midsummer to me; no ripeness or maturity in nature yet.   The grass very

tender and succulent, the streams full and roily.
Yarrow and cinquefoil also in the grass where I sit.
The plantain in bloom and fragrant. Along the
Avon, the meadow-sweet in full bloom, with a fine
cinnamon odor. A wild rose here and there in the
hedge-rows. The wild clematis nearly ready to
bloom, in appearance almost identical with our own.
The wheat and oats full-grown, but not yet turning.
The clouds soft and fleecy. Prunella dark purple.
A few paces farther on I enter a highway, one of
the broadest I have seen, the roadbed hard and
smooth as usual, about sixteen feet wide, with
grassy margins twelve feet wide, redolent with
white and red clover. A rich farming landscape
spreads around me, with blue hills in the far west.
Cool and fresh like June. Bumblebees here and
there, more hairy than at home. A plow in a field
by the roadside is so heavy I can barely move it,
— at least three times as heavy as an American
plow; beam very long, tails four inches square, the
mould-board a thick plank. The soil like putty;
where it dries, crumbling into small, hard lumps,
but sticky and tough when damp, — Shakespeare's
soil, — the finest and most versatile wit of the world,
the product of a sticky, stubborn clay-bank! Here
is a field where every alternate swell is small. The
large swells heave up in a very molten-like way —
real turfy billows, crested with white clover-blos-
soms."

"*July* 17. On the road to Warwick, two miles
from Stratford. Morning bright, with sky full of

white, soft, high-piled thunderheads. Plenty of
pink blackberry blossoms along the road; herb
Robert in bloom, and a kind of Solomon's-seal as
at home, and what appears to be a species of golden-
rod with a midsummery smell. The note of the
yellow-hammer and the wren here and there. Beech-
trees loaded with mast and humming with bumblebees, probably gathering honey-dew, which seems
to be more abundant here than with us. The landscape like a well-kept park dotted with great trees,
which make islands of shade in a sea of grass.
Droves of sheep grazing, and herds of cattle reposing in the succulent fields. Now the just felt
breeze brings me the rattle of a mowing-machine, a
rare sound here, as most of the grass is cut by hand.
The great motionless arms of a windmill rising here
and there above the horizon. A gentleman's turn-
out goes by with glittering wheels and spanking
team; the footman in livery behind, the gentleman
driving. I hear his brake scrape as he puts it on
down the gentle descent. Now a lark goes off.
Then the mellow horn of a cow or heifer is heard.
Then the bleat of sheep. The crows caw hoarsely.
Few houses by the roadside, but here and there
behind the trees in the distance. I hear the greenfinch, stronger and sharper than our goldfinch, but
less pleasing. The matured look of some fields of
grass alone suggests midsummer. Several species of
mint by the roadside, also certain white umbelliferous plants. Everywhere that royal weed of Britain the nettle. Shapely piles of road material and

pounded stone at regular distances, every fragment
of which will go through a two-inch ring. The
roads are mended only in winter, and are kept as
smooth and hard as a rock. No swells or 'thank-
y'-ma'ams' in them to turn the water; they shed
the water like a rounded pavement. On the hill,
three miles from Stratford, where a finger-post points
you to Hampton Lucy, I turn and see the spire of
Shakespeare's church between the trees. It lies in
a broad, gentle valley, and rises above much foliage.
'I hope and praise God it will keep foine,' said the
old woman at whose little cottage I stopped for
ginger-beer, attracted by a sign in the window.
'One penny, sir, if you please. I made it myself,
sir. I do not leave the front door unfastened'
(undoing it to let me out) 'when I am down in the
garden.' A weasel runs across the road in front of
me, and is scolded by a little bird. The body of
a dead hedgehog festering beside the hedge. A
species of St. John's-wort in bloom, teasels, and a
small convolvulus. Also a species of plantain with
a head large as my finger, purple tinged with white.
Road margins wide, grassy, and fragrant with
clover. Privet in bloom in the hedges, panicles of
small white flowers faintly sweet-scented. 'As
clean and white as privet when it flowers,' says
Tennyson in 'Walking to the Mail.' The road
and avenue between noble trees, beech, ash, elm,
and oak. All the fields are bounded by lines of
stately trees; the distance is black with them. A
large thistle by the roadside, with homeless bumble-

bees on the heads as at home, some of them white-faced and stingless. Thistles rare in this country. Weeds of all kinds rare except the nettle. The place to see the Scotch thistle is not in Scotland or England, but in America."

III

England is like the margin of a spring-run near its source, — always green, always cool, always moist, comparatively free from frost in winter and from drought in summer. The spring-run to which it owes this character is the Gulf Stream, which brings out of the pit of the southern ocean what the fountain brings out of the bowels of the earth — a uniform temperature, low but constant; a fog in winter, a cloud in summer. The spirit of gentle, fertilizing summer rain perhaps never took such tangible and topographical shape before. Cloud-evolved, cloud-enveloped, cloud-protected, it fills the eye of the American traveler with a vision of greenness such as he has never before dreamed of; a greenness born of perpetual May, tender, untarnished, ever renewed, and as uniform and all-pervading as the rain-drops that fall, covering mountain, cliff, and vale alike. The softened, rounded, flowing outlines given to our landscape by a deep fall of snow are given to the English by this depth of vegetable mould and this all-prevailing verdure which it supports. Indeed, it is caught upon the shelves and projections of the rocks as if it fell from the clouds, — a kind of green snow, — and it clings to their rough or slanting sides like moist flakes. In the little valleys and chasms it appears to lie deepest. Only the peaks and broken rocky crests of the highest Scotch and Cumberland mountains are bare. Adown their treeless sides the moist, fresh greenness fairly drips. Grass, grass, grass, and evermore grass. Is there another country under the sun so becushioned, becarpeted, and becurtained with grass? Even the woods are full of grass, and I have seen them mowing in a forest. Grass grows upon the rocks, upon the walls, on the tops of the old castles, on the roofs of the houses, and in winter the hay-seed sometimes sprouts upon the backs of the sheep. Turf used as capping to a stone fence thrives and blooms as if upon the ground. There seems to be a deposit from the atmosphere, — a slow but steady accumulation of a black, peaty mould upon all exposed surfaces, — that by and by supports some of the lower or cryptogamous forms of vegetation. These decay and add to the soil, till thus in time grass and other plants will grow. The walls of the old castles and cathedrals support a variety of plant life. On Rochester Castle I saw two or three species of large wild flowers growing one hundred feet from the ground and tempting the tourist to perilous reachings and climbings to get them. The very stones seem to sprout. My companion made a sketch of a striking group of red and white flowers blooming far up on one of the buttresses of Rochester Cathedral. The soil will climb to any height. Indeed,

there seems to be a kind of finer soil floating in the
air. How else can one account for the general
smut of the human face and hands in this country,
and the impossibility of keeping his own clean?
The unwashed hand here quickly leaves its mark
on whatever it touches. A prolonged neglect of
soap and water, and I think one would be presently
covered with a fine green mould, like that upon
the boles of the trees in the woods. If the rains
were not occasionally heavy enough to clean them
off, I have no doubt that the roofs of all buildings
in England would in a few years be covered with
turf, and that daisies and buttercups would bloom
upon them. How quickly all new buildings take
on the prevailing look of age and mellowness!
One needs to have seen the great architectural piles
and monuments of Britain to appreciate Shakespeare's line, —

> "That unswept stone, besmeared with sluttish Time."

He must also have seen those Scotch or Cumberland
mountains to appreciate the descriptive force of this
other line, —

> "The turfy mountains where live the nibbling sheep."

The turfy mountains are the unswept stones that
have held and utilized their ever-increasing capital
of dirt. These vast rocky eminences are stuffed
and padded with peat; it is the sooty soil of the
housetops and of the grimy human hand, deepened
and accumulated till it nourishes the finest, sweetest
grass.

It was this turfy and grassy character of these

mountains — I am tempted to say their cushiony character — that no reading or picture viewing of mine had prepared me for. In the cut or on canvas they appeared like hard and frowning rocks; and here I beheld them as green and succulent as any meadow-bank in April or May, — vast, elevated sheep-walks and rabbit-warrens, treeless, shrubless, generally without loose bowlders, shelving rocks, or sheer precipices; often rounded, feminine, dimpled, or impressing one as if the rock had been thrust up beneath an immense stretch of the finest lawn, and had carried the turf with it heavenward, rending it here and there, but preserving acres of it intact.

In Scotland I ascended Ben Venue, not one of the highest or ruggedest of the Scotch mountains, but a fair sample of them, and my foot was seldom off the grass or bog, often sinking into them as into a saturated sponge. Where I expected a dry course, I found a wet one. The thick, springy turf was oozing with water. Instead of being balked by precipices, I was hindered by swamps. Where a tangle of brush or a chaos of bowlders should have detained me, I was picking my way as through a wet meadow-bottom tilted up at an angle of forty-five degrees. My feet became soaked when my shins should have been bruised. Occasionally, a large deposit of peat in some favored place had given way beneath the strain of much water, and left a black chasm a few yards wide and a yard or more deep. Cold spring-runs were abundant, wild flowers few, grass universal. A loping hare started up before me; a pair of ringed ousels took a hasty glance at me from behind a rock; sheep and lambs, the latter white and conspicuous beside their dingy and all but invisible dams, were scattered here and there; the wheat-ear uncovered its white rump as it flitted from rock to rock, and the mountain pipit displayed its larklike tail. No sound of wind in the trees; there were no trees, no seared branches and trunks that so enhance and set off the wildness of our mountain-tops. On the summit the wind whistled around the outcropping rocks and hummed among the heather, but the great mountain did not purr or roar like one covered with forests.

I lingered for an hour or more, and gazed upon the stretch of mountain and vale about me. The summit of Ben Lomond, eight or ten miles to the west, rose a few hundred feet above me. On four peaks I could see snow or miniature glaciers. Only four or five houses, mostly humble shepherd dwellings, were visible in that wide circuit. The sun shone out at intervals; the driving clouds floated low, their keels scraping the rocks of some of the higher summits. The atmosphere was filled with a curious white film, like water tinged with milk, an effect only produced at home by a fine mist. "A certain tameness in the view, after all," I recorded in my note-book on the spot, "perhaps because of the trim and grassy character of the mountain; not solemn and impressive; no sense of age or power. The rock crops out everywhere, but it can hardly look you in the face; it is crumbling and insignificant; shows no frowning walls, no tremendous cleavage; nothing overhanging and precipitous; no wrath and revel of the elder gods."

Even in rugged Scotland nature is scarcely wilder than a mountain sheep, certainly a good way short of the ferity of the moose and caribou. There is everywhere marked repose and moderation in the scenery, a kind of aboriginal Scotch canniness and propriety that gives one a new sensation. On and about Ben Nevis there is barrenness, cragginess, and desolation; but the characteristic feature of wild Scotch scenery is the moor, lifted up into mountains, covering low, broad hills, or stretching away in undulating plains, black, silent, melancholy, it may be, but never savage or especially wild. "The vast and yet not savage solitude," Carlyle says, referring to these moorlands. The soil is black and peaty, often boggy; the heather short and uniform as prairie grass; a shepherd's cottage or a sportsman's "box" stuck here and there amid the hills. The highland cattle are shaggy and picturesque, but the moors and mountains are close cropped and uniform. The solitude is not that of a forest full of still forms and dim vistas, but of wide, open, sombre spaces. Nature did not look alien or unfriendly to me; there must be barrenness or some savage threatening feature in the landscape to produce this impression; but the heather and whin are like a permanent shadow, and one longs to see the trees stand up and wave their branches. The torrents leaping down off the mountains are

very welcome to both eye and ear. And the lakes
— nothing can be prettier than Loch Lomond and
Loch Katrine, though one wishes for some of the
superfluous rocks of the New World to give their
beauty a granite setting.

IV

It is characteristic of nature in England that
most of the stone with which the old bridges,
churches, and cathedrals are built is so soft that
people carve their initials in it with their jack-
knives, as we do in the bark of a tree or in a piece
of pine timber. At Stratford a card has been
posted upon the outside of the old church, implor-
ing visitors to refrain from this barbarous practice.
One sees names and dates there more than a century
old. Often, in leaning over the parapets of the
bridges along the highways, I would find them covered with letters and figures. Tourists have made
such havoc chipping off fragments from the old
Brig o' Doon in Burns's country, that the parapet
has had to be repaired. One could cut out the key of
the arch with his pocket-knife. And yet these old
structures outlast empires. A few miles from Glasgow I saw the remains of an old Roman bridge, the
arch apparently as perfect as when the first Roman
chariot passed over it, probably fifteen centuries
ago. No wheels but those of time pass over it in
these later centuries, and these seem to be driven
slowly and gently in this land, with but little wear
and tear to the ancient highways.

England is not a country of granite and marble, but of chalk, marl, and clay. The old Plutonic gods do not assert themselves; they are buried and turned to dust, and the more modern humanistic divinities bear sway. The land is a green cemetery of extinct rude forces. Where the highway or the railway gashed the hills deeply, I could seldom tell where the soil ended and the rock began, as they gradually assimilated, blended, and became one.

And this is the key to nature in England: 't is granite grown ripe and mellow and issuing in grass and verdure; 't is aboriginal force and fecundity become docile and equable and mounting toward higher forms, — the harsh, bitter rind of the earth grown sweet and edible. There is such body and substance in the color and presence of things that one thinks the very roots of the grass must go deeper than usual. The crude, the raw, the discordant, where are they? It seems a comparatively short and easy step from nature to the canvas or to the poem in this cozy land. Nothing need be added; the idealization has already taken place. The Old World is deeply covered with a kind of human leaf-mould, while the New is for the most part yet raw, undigested hard-pan. This is why these scenes haunt one like a memory. One seems to have youthful associations with every field and hilltop he looks upon. The complete humanization of nature has taken place. The soil has been mixed with human thought and substance. These fields have been alternately Celt, Roman, British, Nor-

man, Saxon; they have moved and walked and
talked and loved and suffered; hence one feels kindred to them and at home among them. The
mother-land, indeed. Every foot of its soil has
given birth to a human being and grown tender and
conscious with time.

England is like a seat by the chimney-corner,
and is as redolent of human occupancy and domesticity. It has the island coziness and unity, and
the island simplicity as opposed to the continental
diversity of forms. It is all one neighborhood; a
friendly and familiar air is over all. It satisfies to
the full one's utmost craving for the home-like and
for the fruits of affectionate occupation of the soil.
It does not satisfy one's craving for the wild, the
savage, the aboriginal, what our poet describes
as his

"Hungering, hungering, hungering for primal energies and
Nature's dauntlessness."

But probably in the matter of natural scenes we
hunger most for that which we most do feed upon.
At any rate, I can conceive that one might be easily
contented with what the English landscape affords
him.

The whole physiognomy of the land bespeaks
the action of slow, uniform, conservative agencies.
There is an elemental composure and moderation in
things that leave their mark everywhere, — a sort
of elemental sweetness and docility that are a surprise and a charm. One does not forget that the
evolution of man probably occurred in this hemi-

sphere, and time would seem to have proved that there is something here more favorable to his perpetuity and longevity.

The dominant impression of the English landscape is repose. Never was such a restful land to the eye, especially to the American eye, sated as it is very apt to be with the mingled squalor and splendor of its own landscape, its violent contrasts, and general spirit of unrest. But the completeness and composure of this outdoor nature is like a dream. It is like the poise of the tide at its full: every hurt of the world is healed, every shore covered, every unsightly spot is hidden. The circle of the horizon is brimming with the green equable flood. (I did not see the fens of Lincolnshire nor the wolds of York.) This look of repose is partly the result of the maturity and ripeness brought about by time and ages of patient and thorough husbandry, and partly the result of the gentle, continent spirit of Nature herself. She is contented, she is happily wedded, she is well clothed and fed. Her offspring swarm about her, her paths have fallen in pleasant places. The foliage of the trees, how dense and massive! The turf of the fields, how thick and uniform! The streams and rivers, how placid and full, showing no devastated margins, no widespread sandy wastes and unsightly heaps of drift bowlders! To the returned traveler the foliage of the trees and groves of New England and New York looks thin and disheveled when compared with the foliage he has just left. This effect is probably owing to our cruder soil and sharper climate. The aspect of our trees in midsummer is as if the hair of their heads stood on end; the woods have a wild, frightened look, or as if they were just recovering from a debauch. In our intense light and heat, the leaves, instead of spreading themselves full to the sun and crowding out upon the ends of the branches as they do in England, retreat, as it were, hide behind each other, stand edgewise, perpendicular, or at any angle, to avoid the direct rays. In Britain, from the slow, dripping rains and the excessive moisture, the leaves of the trees droop more, and the branches are more pendent. The rays of light are fewer and feebler, and the foliage disposes itself so as to catch them all, and thus presents a fuller and broader surface to the eye of the beholder. The leaves are massed upon the outer ends of the branches, while the interior of the tree is comparatively leafless. The European plane-tree is like a tent. The foliage is all on the outside. The bird voices in it reverberate as in a chamber.

"The pillar'd dusk of sounding sycamores,"

says Tennyson. At a little distance, it has the mass and solidity of a rock. The same is true of the European maple, and when this tree is grown on our side of the Atlantic it keeps up its Old World habits. I have for several years taken note of a few of them growing in a park near my home. They have less grace and delicacy of outline than our native maple, but present a darker and more

solid mass of foliage. The leaves are larger and less
feathery, and are crowded to the periphery of the
tree. Nearly every summer one of the trees, which
is most exposed, gets the leaves on one side badly
scorched. When the foliage begins to turn in the
fall, the trees appear as if they had been lightly
and hastily brushed with gold. The outer edges of
the branches become a light yellow, while, a little
deeper, the body of the foliage is still green. It is
this solid and sculpturesque character of the English
foliage that so fills the eye of the artist. The
feathery, formless, indefinite, not to say thin, aspect
of our leafage is much less easy to paint, and much
less pleasing when painted.

The same is true of the turf in the fields and
upon the hills. The sward with us, even in the
oldest meadows, will wear more or less a ragged,
uneven aspect. The frost heaves it, the sun parches
it; it is thin here and thick there, crabbed in one
spot and fine and soft in another. Only by the
frequent use of a heavy roller, copious waterings,
and top-dressings, can we produce sod that approaches in beauty even that of the elevated sheep
ranges in England and Scotland.

The greater activity and abundance of the earthworm, as disclosed by Darwin, probably has much
to do with the smoothness and fatness of those
fields when contrasted with our own. This little yet
mighty engine is much less instrumental in leaven-
ing and leveling the soil in New England than in
Old. The greater humidity of the mother country,

the deep clayey soil, its fattening for ages by
human occupancy, the abundance of food, the milder
climate, etc., are all favorable to the life and activity of the earthworm. Indeed, according to Darwin, the gardener that has made England a garden
is none other than this little obscure creature. It
plows, drains, airs, pulverizes, fertilizes, and levels.
It cannot transport rocks and stone, but it can bury
them; it cannot remove the ancient walls and pave-
ments, but it can undermine them and deposit its
rich castings above them. On each acre of land,
he says, "in many parts of England, a weight of
more than ten tons of dry earth annually passes
through their bodies and is brought to the surface."
"When we behold a wide, turf-covered expanse,"
he further observes, "we should remember that its
smoothness, on which so much of its beauty de-
pends, is mainly due to all the inequalities having
been slowly leveled by worms."

The small part which worms play in this direction in our landscape is, I am convinced, more than
neutralized by our violent or disrupting climate;
but England looks like the product of some such
gentle, tireless, and beneficent agent. I have referred to that effect in the face of the landscape as
if the soil had snowed down; it seems the snow
came from the other direction, namely, from below,
but was deposited with equal gentleness and uniformity.

The repose and equipoise of nature of which I
have spoken appears in the fields of grain no less

than in the turf and foliage. One may see vast
stretches of wheat, oats, barley, beans, etc., as uniform as the surface of a lake, every stalk of grain
or bean the size and height of every other stalk.
This, of course, means good husbandry; it means
a mild, even-tempered nature back of it, also.
Then the repose of the English landscape is enhanced, rather than marred, by the part man has
played in it. How those old arched bridges rest
above the placid streams; how easily they conduct
the trim, perfect highways over them! Where
the foot finds an easy way, the eye finds the same;
where the body finds harmony, the mind finds harmony. Those ivy-covered walls and ruins, those
finished fields, those rounded hedge-rows, those
embowered cottages, and that gray, massive architecture, all contribute to the harmony and to the
repose of the landscape. Perhaps in no other
country are the grazing herds so much at ease.
One's first impression, on seeing British fields in
spring or summer, is that the cattle and sheep have
all broken into the meadow and have not yet been
discovered by the farmer; they have taken their
fill, and are now reposing upon the grass or dream-
ing under the trees. But you presently perceive
that it is all meadow or meadow-like; that there
are no wild, weedy, or barren pastures about which
the herds toil; but that they are in grass up to
their eyes everywhere. Hence their contentment;
hence another element of repose in the landscape.

The softness and humidity of the English climate.

act in two ways in promoting that marvelous greenness of the land, namely, by growth and by decay.
As the grass springs quickly, so its matured stalk
or dry leaf decays quickly. No field growths are
desiccated and preserved as with us; there are no
dried stubble and seared leaves remaining over the
winter to mar and obscure the verdancy of spring.
Every dead thing is quickly converted back to vegetable mould. In the woods, in May, it is difficult
to find any of the dry leaves of the previous
autumn; in the fields and copses and along the
highways, no stalk of weed or grass remains; while
our wild, uplying pastures and mountain-tops always
present a more or less brown and seared appearance
from the dried and bleached stalks of the growth of
the previous year, through which the fresh springing grass is scarcely visible. Where rain falls on
nearly three hundred days in the year, as in the
British islands, the conversion of the mould into
grass, and *vice versa*, takes place very rapidly.

II

ENGLISH WOODS: A CONTRAST

ONE cannot well overpraise the rural and pas·
toral beauty of England — the beauty of her
fields, parks, downs, holms. In England you shall
see at its full that of which you catch only glimpses
in this country, the broad, beaming, hospitable
beauty of a perfectly cultivated landscape. Indeed,
to see England is to take one's fill of the orderly,
the permanent, the well-kept in the works of man,
and of the continent, the beneficent, the uniform,
in the works of nature. It is to see the most perfect bit of garden lawn extended till it covers an
empire; it is to see the history of two thousand
years written in grass and verdure, and in the lines
of the landscape; a continent concentrated into a
state, the deserts and waste places left out, every
rood of it swarming with life; the pith and marrow
of wide tracts compacted into narrow fields and
recruited and forwarded by the most vigilant husbandry. Those fields look stall-fed, those cattle
beam contentment, those rivers have never left
their banks; those mountains are the paradise of
shepherds; those open forest glades, half sylvan,
half pastoral, clean, stately, full of long vistas and

cathedral-like aisles, — where else can one find beauty like that? The wild and the savage flee away. The rocks pull the green turf over them like coverlids; the hills are plump with vegetable mould, and when they bend this way or that, their sides are wrinkled and dimpled like the forms of fatted sheep. And fatted they are; not merely by the care of man, but by the elements themselves; the sky rains fertility upon them; there is no wear and tear as with our alternately flooded, parched, and frozen hilltops; the soil accumulates, the mould deepens; the matted turf binds it and yearly adds to it.

All this is not simply because man is or has been so potent in the landscape (this is but half the truth), but because the very mood and humor of Nature herself is domestic and human. She seems to have grown up with man and taken on his look and ways. Her spirit is that of the full, placid stream that you may lead through your garden or conduct by your doorstep without other danger than a wet sill or a soaked flower-plot, at rare intervals. It is the opulent nature of the southern seas, brought by the Gulf Stream, and reproduced and perpetuated here under these cool northern skies, the fangs and the poison taken out; full, but no longer feverish; lusty, but no longer lewd.

Yet there is a certain beauty of nature to be had in much fuller measure in our own country than in England, — the beauty of the wild, the aboriginal, — the beauty of primitive forests, — the beauty of lichen-covered rocks and ledges. The lichen is one of the lowest and humblest forms of vegetable growth, but think how much it adds to the beauty of all our wild scenery, giving to our mountain walls and drift bowlders the softest and most pleasing tints. The rocky escarpments of New York and New England hills are frescoed by Time himself, painted as with the brush of the eternal elements. But the lichen is much less conspicuous in England, and plays no such part in her natural scenery. The climate is too damp. The rocks in Wales and Northumberland and in Scotland are dark and cold and unattractive. The trees in the woods do not wear the mottled suit of soft gray ours do. The bark of the British beech is smooth and close-fitting, and often tinged with a green mould. The Scotch pine is clad as in a ragged suit of leather. Nature uses mosses instead of lichens. The old walls and housetops are covered with moss — a higher form of vegetation than lichens. Its decay soon accumulates a little soil or vegetable mould, which presently supports flowering plants.

Neither are there any rocks in England worth mentioning; no granite bowlders, no fern-decked or moss-covered fragments scattered through the woods, as with us. They have all been used up for building purposes, or for road-making, or else have quite dissolved in the humid climate. I saw rocks in Wales, quite a profusion of them in the pass of Llanberis, but they were tame indeed in comparison with such rock scenery as that say at Lake Mohunk,

in the Shawangunk range in New York. There
are passes in the Catskills that for the grandeur of
wildness and savageness far surpass anything the
Welsh mountains have to show. Then for exquisite and thrilling beauty, probably one of our mottled rocky walls with the dicentra blooming from
little niches and shelves in April, and the columbine thrusting out from seams and crevices clusters
of its orange bells in May, with ferns and mosses
clinging here and there, and the woodbine tracing
a delicate green line across its face, cannot be
matched anywhere in the world.

Then, in our woods, apart from their treasures
of rocks, there is a certain beauty and purity unknown in England, a certain delicacy and sweetness,
and charm of unsophisticated nature, that are native
to our forests.

The pastoral or field life of nature in England is
so rank and full, that no woods or forests that I
was able to find could hold their own against it
for a moment. It flooded them like a tide. The
grass grows luxuriantly in the thick woods, and
where the grass fails, the coarse bracken takes its
place. There was no wood spirit, no wild wood
air. Our forests shut their doors against the fields;
they shut out the strong light and the heat. Where
the land has been long cleared, the woods put out
a screen of low branches, or else a brushy growth
starts up along their borders that guards and protects their privacy. Lift or part away these branches,
and step inside, and you are in another world; new

plants, new flowers, new birds, new animals, new
insects, new sounds, new odors; in fact, an entirely
different atmosphere and presence. Dry leaves cover
the ground, delicate ferns and mosses drape the
rocks, shy, delicate flowers gleam out here and
there, the slender brown wood-frog leaps nimbly
away from your feet, the little red newt fills its
infantile pipe, or hides under a leaf, the ruffed
grouse bursts up before you, the gray squirrel leaps
from tree to tree, the wood pewee utters its plaintive cry, the little warblers lisp and dart amid the
branches, and sooner or later the mosquito demands
his fee.   Our woods suggest new arts, new pleasures, a new mode of life.   English parks and
groves, when the sun shines, suggest a perpetual
picnic, or Maying party; but no one, I imagine,
thinks of camping out in English woods.   The
constant rains, the darkened skies, the low temperature, make the interior of a forest as uninviting as
an underground passage.   I wondered what became
of the dry leaves that are such a feature and give
out such a pleasing odor in our woods.   They are
probably raked up and carried away; or, if left upon
the ground, are quickly resolved into mould by the
damp climate.

While in Scotland I explored a large tract of
woodland, mainly of Scotch fir, that covers a hill
near Ecclefechan, but it was grassy and uninviting.
In one of the parks of the Duke of Hamilton, I
found a deep wooded gorge through which flowed
the river Avon (I saw four rivers of this name in

Great Britain), a branch of the Clyde, — a dark,
rock-paved stream, the color of brown stout. It
was the wildest bit of forest scenery I saw anywhere. I almost imagined myself on the head-
waters of the Hudson or the Penobscot. The stillness, the solitude, the wild boiling waters, were
impressive; but the woods had no charm; there
were no flowers, no birds; the sylvan folk had
moved away long ago, and their house was cold and
inhospitable. I sat a half-hour in their dark nettle-
grown halls by the verge of the creek, to see if they
were stirring anywhere, but they were not. I did,
indeed, hear part of a wren's song, and the call of
the sandpiper; but that was all. Not one purely
wood voice or sound or odor. But looking into the
air a few yards below me, there leapt one of those
matchless stone bridges, clearing the profound gulf
and carrying the road over as securely as if upon
the geological strata. It was the bow of art and
civilization set against nature's wildness. In the
woods beyond, I came suddenly upon the ruins of
an old castle, with great trees growing out of it,
and rabbits burrowing beneath it. One learns that
it takes more than a collection of trees to make a
forest, as we know it in this country. Unless they
house that spirit of wildness and purity like a
temple, they fail to satisfy. In walking to Selborne, I skirted Wolmer Forest, but it had an uninviting look. The Hanger on the hill above Selborne, which remains nearly as it was in White's
time, — a thrifty forest of beeches, — I explored,

phanerogamous - flowering plant

cryptogamous - non flowering plant

stamen stalk filament and pollen bearing portion anther

but found it like the others, without any distinctive
woodsy attraction — only so much soil covered with
dripping beeches, too dense for a park and too tame
for a forest. The soil is a greasy, slippery clay,
and down the steepest part of the hill, amid the
trees, the boys have a slide that serves them for
summer "coastings." Hardly a leaf, hardly a twig
or branch, to be found. In White's time, the poor
people used to pick up the sticks the crows dropped
in building their nests, and they probably do so
yet. When one comes upon the glades beyond the
Hanger, the mingling of groves and grassy common,
the eye is fully content. The beech, which is the
prevailing tree here, as it is in many other parts of
England, is a much finer tree than the American
beech. The deep limestone soil seems especially
adapted to it. It grows as large as our elm, with
much the same manner of branching. The trunk
is not patched and mottled with gray, like ours,
but is often tinged with a fine deep green mould.
The beeches that stand across the road in front of
Wordsworth's house, at Rydal Mount, have boles
nearly as green as the surrounding hills. The bark
of this tree is smooth and close-fitting, and shows
that muscular, athletic character of the tree beneath
it which justifies Spenser's phrase, "the warlike
beech." These beeches develop finely in the open,
and make superb shade-trees along the highway.
All the great historical forests of England — Shrews-
bury Forest, the Forest of Dean, New Forest, etc.
— have practically disappeared. Remnants of them

remain here and there, but the country they once occupied is now essentially pastoral.

It is noteworthy that there is little or no love of woods as such in English poetry; no fond mention of them, and dwelling upon them. The muse of Britain's rural poetry has none of the wide-eyedness and furtiveness of the sylvan creatures; she is rather a gentle, wholesome, slightly stupid divinity of the fields. Milton sings the praises of

> " Arched walks of twilight groves."

But his wood is a "drear wood,"

> " The nodding horror of whose shady brows
> Threats the forlorn and wandering passenger."

Again: —

> " Very desolation dwells
> By grots and caverns shagg'd with horrid shade."

Shakespeare refers to the "ruthless, vast, and horrid wood," — a fit place for robbery, rapine, and murder. Indeed, English poetry is pretty well colored with the memory of the time when the woods were the hiding-places of robbers and outlaws, and were the scenes of all manner of dark deeds. The only thing I recall in Shakespeare that gives a faint whiff of our forest life occurs in "All 's Well That Ends Well," where the clown says to Lafeu, "I am a woodland fellow, sir, that always loved a great fire." That great fire is American; wood is too scarce in Europe. Francis Higginson wrote in 1630: "New England may boast of the element of fire more than all the rest; for all Europe is not able to afford to make so great fires as New England. A poor servant, that is to possess but fifty acres, may afford to give more wood for fire, as good as the world yields, than many noblemen in England." In many parts of New England, New York, and Pennsylvania, the same royal fires may still be indulged in. In the chief nature-poet of England, Wordsworth, there is no line that has the subtle aroma of the deep woods. After seeing his country, one can recognize its features, its spirit, all through his poems — its impressive solitudes, its lonely tarns, its silent fells, its green dales, its voiceful waterfalls; but there are no woods there to speak of; the mountains appear to have always been treeless, and the poet's muse has never felt the spell of this phase of nature — the mystery and attraction of the indoors of aboriginal wildness. Likewise in Tennyson there is the breath of the wold, but not of the woods.

Among our own poets, two at least of the more eminent have listened to the siren of our primitive woods. I refer to Bryant and Emerson. Though so different, there is an Indian's love of forests and forest-solitudes in them both. Neither Bryant's "Forest Hymn" nor Emerson's "Woodnotes" could have been written by an English poet. The "Woodnotes" savor of our vast Northern pine forests, amid which one walks with distended pupil, and a boding, alert sense.

> "In unploughed Maine he sought the lumberers' gang,
> Where from a hundred lakes young rivers sprang;
> He trode the unplanted forest floor, whereon
> The all-seeing sun for ages hath not shone;

Where feeds the moose, and walks the surly bear,
And up the tall mast runs the woodpecker.
He saw beneath dim aisles, in odorous beds,
The slight Linnæa hang its twin-born heads,
And blessed the monument of the man of flowers,
Which breathes his sweet fame through the northern bowers.
He heard, when in the grove, at intervals,
With sudden roar the aged pine-tree falls, —
One crash, the death-hymn of the perfect tree,
Declares the close of its green century."

Emerson's muse is urbane, but it is that wise
urbanity that is at home in the woods as well as in
the town, and can make a garden of a forest.

" My garden is a forest ledge,
    Which older forests bound;
The banks slope down to the blue lake-edge,
    Then plunge to depths profound."

On the other hand, we have no pastoral poetry
in the English sense, because we have no pastoral
nature as overpowering as the English have. When
the muse of our poetry is not imitative, it often
has a piny, woodsy flavor, that is unknown in the
older literatures. The gentle muse of Longfellow,
so civil, so cultivated; yet how it delighted in all
legends and echoes and Arcadian dreams, that date
from the forest primeval. Thoreau was a wood-
genius — the spirit of some Indian poet or prophet,
graduated at Harvard College, but never losing his
taste for the wild. The shy, mystical genius of
Hawthorne was never more at home than when in
the woods. Read the forest-scenes in the " Scarlet
Letter." They are among the most suggestive in
the book.

IN CARLYLE'S COUNTRY

IN crossing the sea a second time, I was more curious to see Scotland than England, partly because I had had a good glimpse of the latter country eleven years before, but largely because I had always preferred the Scotch people to the English (I had seen and known more of them in my youth), and especially because just then I was much absorbed with Carlyle, and wanted to see with my own eyes the land and the race from which he sprang.

I suspect anyhow I am more strongly attracted by the Celt than by the Anglo-Saxon; at least by the individual Celt. Collectively the Anglo-Saxon is the more impressive; his triumphs are greater; the face of his country and of his cities is the more pleasing; the gift of empire is his. Yet there can be no doubt, I think, that the Celts, at least the Scotch Celts, are a more hearty, cordial, and hospitable people than the English; they have more curiosity, more raciness, and quicker and surer sympathies. They fuse and blend readily with another people, which the English seldom do. In this country John Bull is usually like a pebble in the clay; grind him and press him and bake him as you will, he is still a pebble — a hard spot in the brick, but not essentially a part of it.

Every close view I got of the Scotch character confirmed my liking for it. A most pleasant episode happened to me down in Ayr. A young man whom I stumbled on by chance in a little wood by the Doon, during some conversation about the birds that were singing around us, quoted my own name to me. This led to an acquaintance with the family and with the parish minister, and gave a genuine human coloring to our brief sojourn in Burns's country. In Glasgow I had an inside view of a household a little lower in the social scale, but high in the scale of virtues and excellences. I climbed up many winding stone stairs and found the family in three or four rooms on the top floor: a father, mother, three sons, two of them grown, and a daughter, also grown. The father and the sons worked in an iron foundry near by. I broke bread with them around the table in the little cluttered kitchen, and was spared apologies as much as if we had been seated at a banquet in a baronial hall. A Bible chapter was read after we were seated at table, each member of the family reading a verse alternately. When the meal was over, we went into the next room, where all joined in singing some Scotch songs, mainly from Burns. One of the sons possessed the finest bass voice I had ever listened to. Its power was simply tremendous, well tempered with the Scotch raciness and tenderness, too. He had taken the first prize at a public singing bout, open to competition to all of Scotland. I told his mother, who also had a voice of wonderful sweetness, that such a gift would make her son's fortune anywhere, and found that the subject was the cause of much anxiety to her. She feared lest it should be the ruination of him — lest he should prostitute it to the service of the devil, as she put it, rather than use it to the glory of God. She said she had rather follow him to his grave than see him in the opera or concert hall, singing for money. She wanted him to stick to his work, and use his voice only as a pious and sacred gift. When I asked the young man to come and sing for us at the hotel, the mother was greatly troubled, as she afterward told me, till she learned we were stopping at a temperance house. But the young man seemed not at all inclined to break away from the advice of his mother. The other son had a sweetheart who had gone to America, and he was looking longingly thitherward. He showed me her picture, and did not at all attempt to conceal from me, or from his family, his interest in the original. Indeed, one would have said there were no secrets or concealments in such a family, and the thorough unaffected piety of the whole household, mingled with so much that was human and racy and canny, made an impression upon me I shall not soon forget. This family was probably an exceptional one, but it tinges all my recollections of smoky, tall-chimneyed Glasgow.

A Scotch trait of quite another sort, and more

suggestive of Burns than of Carlyle, was briefly
summarized in an item of statistics which I used to
read in one of the Edinburgh papers every Monday
morning, namely, that of the births registered during the previous week, invariably from ten to twelve
per cent. were illegitimate. The Scotch — all classes
of them — love Burns deep down in their hearts,
because he has expressed them, from the roots up,
as none other has.

When I think of Edinburgh the vision that
comes before my mind's eye is of a city presided
over, and shone upon as it were, by two green treeless heights. Arthur's Seat is like a great irregular
orb or half-orb, rising above the near horizon there
in the southeast, and dominating city and country
with its unbroken verdancy. Its greenness seems
almost to pervade the air itself — a slight radiance
of grass, there in the eastern skies. No description
of Edinburgh I had read had prepared me for the
striking hill features that look down upon it.
There is a series of three hills which culminate in
Arthur's Seat, 800 feet high. Upon the first and
smaller hill stands the Castle. This is a craggy,
precipitous rock, on three sides, but sloping down
into a broad gentle expanse toward the east, where
the old city of Edinburgh is mainly built, — as if
it had flowed out of the Castle as out of a fountain,
and spread over the adjacent ground. Just beyond
the point where it ceases rise Salisbury Crags to a
height of 570 feet, turning to the city a sheer wall
of rocks like the Palisades of the Hudson. From

its brink eastward again, the ground slopes in a broad expanse of greensward to a valley called Hunter's Bog, where I thought the hunters were very quiet and very numerous until I saw they were city riflemen engaged in target practice; thence it rises irregularly to the crest of Arthur's Seat, forming the pastoral eminence and green-shining disk to which I have referred. Along the crest of Salisbury Crags the thick turf comes to the edge of the precipices, as one might stretch a carpet. It is so firm and compact that the boys cut their initials in it, on a large scale, with their jack-knives, as in the bark of a tree. Arthur's Seat was a favorite walk of Carlyle's during those gloomy days in Edinburgh in 1820–21. It was a mount of vision to him, and he apparently went there every day when the weather permitted.[1]

There was no road in Scotland or in England which I should have been so glad to walk over as that from Edinburgh to Ecclefechan, — a distance covered many times by the feet of him whose birth and burial place I was about to visit. Carlyle as a young man had walked it with Edward Irving (the Scotch say "travel" when they mean going afoot), and he had walked it alone, and as a lad with an elder boy, on his way to Edinburgh college. He says in his "Reminiscences" he nowhere else had such affectionate, sad, thoughtful, and, in fact, interesting and salutary journeys. "No company to you but the rustle of the grass under foot, the

[1] See letter to his brother John, March 9, 1821.

tinkling of the brook, or the voices of innocent, primeval things." "I have had days as clear as Italy (as in this Irving case); days moist and dripping, overhung with the infinite of silent gray, — and perhaps the latter were the preferable, in certain moods. You had the world and its waste imbroglios of joy and woe, of light and darkness, to yourself alone. You could strip barefoot, if it suited better; carry shoes and socks over shoulder, hung on your stick; clean shirt and comb were in your pocket; *omnia mea mecum porto.* You lodged with shepherds, who had clean, solid cottages; wholesome eggs, milk, oatmeal porridge, clean blankets to their beds, and a great deal of human sense and unadulterated natural politeness."

But how can one walk a hundred miles in cool blood without a companion, especially when the trains run every hour, and he has a surplus sovereign in his pocket? One saves time and consults his ease by riding, but he thereby misses the real savor of the land. And the roads of this compact little kingdom are so inviting, like a hard, smooth surface covered with sand-paper! How easily the foot puts them behind it! And the summer weather, — what a fresh under-stratum the air has even on the warmest days! Every breath one draws has a cool, invigorating core to it, as if there might be some unmelted, or just melted, frost not far off.

But as we did not walk, there was satisfaction in knowing that the engine which took our train down from Edinburgh was named Thomas Carlyle. The cognomen looked well on the toiling, fiery-hearted, iron-browed monster. I think its original owner would have contemplated it with grim pleasure, especially since he confesses to having spent some time, once, in trying to look up a shipmaster who had named his vessel for him. Here was a hero after his own sort, a leader by the divine right of the expansive power of steam.

The human faculties of observation have not yet adjusted themselves to the flying train. Steam has clapped wings to our shoulders without the power to soar; we get bird's-eye views without the bird's eyes or the bird's elevation, distance without breadth, detail without mass. If such speed only gave us a proportionate extent of view, if this leisure of the eye were only mated to an equal leisure in the glance! Indeed, when one thinks of it, how near railway traveling, as a means of seeing a country, comes, except in the discomforts of it, to being no traveling at all! It is like being tied to your chair, and being jolted and shoved about at home. The landscape is turned topsy-turvy. The eye sustains unnatural relations to all but the most distant objects. We move in an arbitrary plane, and seldom is anything seen from the proper point, or with the proper sympathy of coördinate position. We shall have to wait for the air ship to give us the triumph over space in which the eye can share. Of this flight south from Edinburgh on that bright summer day, I keep only the most general impression. I recall how clean and naked the country looked, lifted up in broad hill-slopes, naked of forests and trees and weedy, bushy growths, and of everything that would hide or obscure its unbroken verdancy, — the one impression that of a universe of grass, as in the arctic regions it might be one of snow; the mountains, pastoral solitudes; the vales, emerald vistas.

Not to be entirely cheated out of my walk, I left the train at Lockerbie, a small Scotch market town, and accomplished the remainder of the journey to Ecclefechan on foot, a brief six-mile pull. It was the first day of June; the afternoon sun was shining brightly. It was still the honeymoon of travel with me, not yet two weeks in the bonnie land; the road was smooth and clean as the floor of a sea beach, and firmer, and my feet devoured the distance with right good will. The first red clover had just bloomed, as I probably should have found it that day had I taken a walk at home; but, like the people I met, it had a ruddier cheek than at home. I observed it on other occasions, and later in the season, and noted that it had more color than in this country, and held its bloom longer. All grains and grasses ripen slower there than here, the season is so much longer and cooler. The pink and ruddy tints are more common in the flowers also. The bloom of the blackberry is often of a decided pink, and certain white, umbelliferous plants, like yarrow, have now and then a rosy tinge. The little white daisy ("gowan," the Scotch call it) is tipped with crimson, foretelling the scarlet poppies, with which the grain fields will by and by be splashed. Prunella (self-heal), also, is of a deeper purple than with us, and a species of cranesbill, like our wild geranium, is of a much deeper and stronger color. On the other hand, their ripened fruits and foliage of autumn pale their ineffectual colors beside our own.

Among the farm occupations, that which most took my eye, on this and on other occasions, was the furrowing of the land for turnips and potatoes; it is done with such absolute precision. It recalled Emerson's statement that the fields in this island look as if finished with a pencil instead of a plow, — a pencil and a ruler in this case, the lines were so straight and so uniform. I asked a farmer at work by the roadside how he managed it. "Ah," said he, "a Scotchman's head is level." Both here and in England, plowing is studied like a fine art; they have plowing matches, and offer prizes for the best furrow. In planting both potatoes and turnips the ground is treated alike, grubbed, plowed, cross-plowed, crushed, harrowed, chain-harrowed, and rolled. Every sod and tuft of uprooted grass is carefully picked up by women and boys, and burned or carted away; leaving the surface of the ground like a clean sheet of paper, upon which the plowman is now to inscribe his perfect lines. The plow is drawn by two horses; it is a long, heavy tool, with double mould-boards, and throws the earth each way. In opening the first furrow the plowman is guided by stakes; having got this one perfect, it is used as the model for every subsequent one, and the land is thrown into ridges as uniform and faultless as if it had been stamped at one stroke with a die, or cast in a mould. It is so from one end of the island to the other; the same expert seems to have done the work in every plowed and planted field.

Four miles from Lockerbie I came to Mainhill, the name of a farm where the Carlyle family lived many years, and where Carlyle first read Goethe, "in a dry ditch," Froude says, and translated "Wilhelm Meister." The land drops gently away to the south and east, opening up broad views in these directions, but it does not seem to be the bleak and windy place Froude describes it. The crops looked good, and the fields smooth and fertile. The soil is rather a stubborn clay, nearly the same as one sees everywhere. A sloping field adjoining the highway was being got ready for turnips. The ridges had been cast; the farmer, a courteous but serious and reserved man, was sprinkling some commercial fertilizer in the furrows from a bag slung across his shoulders, while a boy, with a horse and cart, was depositing stable manure in the same furrows, which a lassie, in clogs and short skirts, was evenly distributing with a fork. Certain work in Scotch fields always seems to be done by women and girls, — spreading manure, pulling weeds, and picking up sods, — while they take an equal hand with the men in the hay and harvest fields.

The Carlyles were living on this farm while their son was teaching school at Annan, and later at Kirkcaldy with Irving, and they supplied him with cheese, butter, ham, oatmeal, etc., from their scanty stores. A new farmhouse has been built since then, though the old one is still standing; doubtless the same Carlyle's father refers to in a letter to his son, in 1817, as being under way. The parish minister was expected at Mainhill. "Your mother was very anxious to have the house done before he came, or else she said she would run over the hill and hide herself."

From Mainhill the highway descends slowly to the village of Ecclefechan, the site of which is marked to the eye, a mile or more away, by the spire of the church rising up against a background of Scotch firs, which clothe a hill beyond. I soon entered the main street of the village, which in Carlyle's youth had an open burn or creek flowing through the centre of it. This has been covered over by some enterprising citizen, and instead of a loitering little burn, crossed by numerous bridges, the eye is now greeted by a broad expanse of small cobble-stone. The cottages are for the most part very humble, and rise from the outer edges of the pavement, as if the latter had been turned up and shaped to make their walls. The church is a handsome brown stone structure, of recent date, and is more in keeping with the fine fertile country about than with the little village in its front. In the cemetery back of it, Carlyle lies buried. As I approached, a girl sat by the roadside, near the gate, combing her black locks and arranging her toilet; waiting, as it proved, for her mother and brother, who lingered in the village. A couple of boys were cutting nettles against the hedge; for the pigs, they said, after the sting had been taken out of them by boiling. Across the street from the cemetery the cows of the villagers were grazing.

I must have thought it would be as easy to distinguish Carlyle's grave from the others as it was to distinguish the man while living, or his fame when dead; for it never occurred to me to ask in what part of the inclosure it was placed. Hence, when I found myself inside the gate, which opens from the Annan road through a high stone wall, I followed the most worn path toward a new and imposing-looking monument on the far side of the cemetery; and the edge of my fine emotion was a good deal dulled against the marble when I found it bore a strange name. I tried others, and still others, but was disappointed. I found a long row of Carlyles, but he whom I sought was not among them. My pilgrim enthusiasm felt itself needlessly hindered and chilled. How many rebuffs could one stand? Carlyle dead, then, was the same as Carlyle living; sure to take you down a peg or two when you came to lay your homage at his feet.

Presently I saw "Thomas Carlyle" on a big marble slab that stood in a family inclosure. But this turned out to be the name of a nephew of the great Thomas. However, I had struck the right plat at last; here were the Carlyles I was looking for, within a space probably of eight by sixteen feet, surrounded by a high iron fence. The latest made grave was higher and fuller than the rest, but it had no stone or mark of any kind to distinguish it. Since my visit, I believe, a stone or monument of some kind has been put up. A few daisies and the pretty blue-eyed speedwell were growing amid the grass upon it The great man lies with his head toward the south or southwest, with his mother, sister, and father to the right of him, and his brother John to the left. I was glad to learn that the high iron fence was not his own suggestion. His father had put it around the family plat in his lifetime. Carlyle would have liked to have it cut down about half way. The whole look of this cemetery, except in the extraordinary size of the headstones, was quite American, it being back of the church, and separated from it, a kind of mortuary garden, instead of surrounding it and running under it, as is the case with the older churches. I noted here, as I did elsewhere, that the custom prevails of putting the trade or occupation of the deceased upon his stone: So-and-So, mason, or tailor, or carpenter, or farmer, etc.

A young man and his wife were working in a nursery of young trees, a few paces from the graves, and I conversed with them through a thin place in the hedge. They said they had seen Carlyle many times, and seemed to hold him in proper esteem and reverence. The young man had seen him come

in summer and stand, with uncovered head, beside
the graves of his father and mother.   "And long
and reverently did he remain there, too," said the
young gardener.   I learned this was Carlyle's inva-
riable custom: every summer did he make a pilgrimage to this spot, and with bared head linger beside
these graves.   The last time he came, which was
a couple of years before he died, he was so feeble
that two persons sustained him while he walked
into the cemetery.   This observance recalls a passage from his "Past and Present."   Speaking of
the religious custom of the Emperor of China, he
says, "He and his three hundred millions (it is
their chief punctuality) visit yearly the Tombs of
their Fathers; each man the Tomb of his Father
and his Mother; alone there in silence with what
of 'worship' or of other thought there may be,
pauses solemnly each man; the divine Skies all
silent over him; the divine Graves, and this divin-
est Grave, all silent under him; the pulsings of his
own soul, if he have any soul, alone audible.   Truly
it may be a kind of worship!   Truly, if a man cannot get some glimpse into the Eternities, looking
through this portal, — through what other need he
try it?"

Carlyle's reverence and affection for his kindred
were among his most beautiful traits, and make up
in some measure for the contempt he felt toward
the rest of mankind.   The family stamp was never
more strongly set upon a man, and no family ever
had a more original, deeply cut pattern than that of

the Carlyles. Generally, in great men who emerge from obscure peasant homes, the genius of the family takes an enormous leap, or is completely metamorphosed; but Carlyle keeps all the paternal lineaments unfaded; he is his father and his mother, touched to finer issues. That wonderful speech of his sire, which all who knew him feared, has lost nothing in the son, but is tremendously augmented, and cuts like a Damascus sword, or crushes like a sledge-hammer. The strongest and finest paternal traits have survived in him. Indeed, a little congenital rill seems to have come all the way down from the old vikings. Carlyle is not merely Scotch; he is Norselandic. There is a marked Scandinavian flavor in him; a touch, or more than a touch, of the rude, brawling, bullying, hard-hitting, wrestling viking times. The hammer of Thor antedates the hammer of his stone-mason sire in him. He is Scotland, past and present, moral and physical. John Knox and the Covenanters survive in him: witness his religious zeal, his depth and solemnity of conviction, his strugglings and agonizings, his "conversion." Ossian survives in him: behold that melancholy retrospect, that gloom, that melodious wail. And especially, as I have said, do his immediate ancestors survive in him, — his sturdy, toiling, fiery-tongued, clannish yeoman progenitors: all are summed up here; this is the net result available for literature in the nineteenth century.

Carlyle's heart was always here in Scotland. A vague, yearning homesickness seemed ever to possess him. "The Hill I first saw the Sun rise over," he says in "Past and Present," "when the Sun and I and all things were yet in their auroral hour, who can divorce me from it? Mystic, deep as the world's centre, are the roots I have struck into my Native Soil; no *tree* that grows is rooted so." How that mournful retrospective glance haunts his pages! His race, generation upon generation, had toiled and wrought here amid the lonely moors, had wrestled with poverty and privation, had wrung the earth for a scanty subsistence, till they had become identified with the soil, kindred with it. How strong the family ties had grown in the struggle; how the sentiment of home was fostered! Then the Carlyles were men who lavished their heart and conscience upon their work; they builded themselves, their days, their thoughts and sorrows, into their houses; they leavened the soil with the sweat of their rugged brows. When James Carlyle, his father, after a lapse of fifty years, saw Auldgarth bridge, upon which he had worked as a lad, he was deeply moved. When Carlyle in his turn saw it, and remembered his father and all he had told him, he also was deeply moved. "It was as if half a century of past time had fatefully for moments turned back." Whatever these men touched with their hands in honest toil became sacred to them, a page out of their own lives. A silent, inarticulate kind of religion they put into their work. All this bore fruit in their distinguished descendant. It gave him that reverted, half mournful gaze; the ground was hallowed behind him; his dead called to him from their graves. Nothing deepens and intensifies family traits like poverty and toil and suffering. It is the furnace heat that brings out the characters, the pressure that makes the strata perfect. One recalls Carlyle's grandmother getting her children up late at night, his father one of them, to break their long fast with oaten cakes from the meal that had but just arrived; making the fire from straw taken from their beds. Surely, such things reach the springs of being.

It seemed eminently fit that Carlyle's dust should rest here in his native soil, with that of his kindred, he was so thoroughly one of them, and that his place should be next his mother's, between whom and himself there existed such strong affection. I recall a little glimpse he gives of his mother in a letter to his brother John, while the latter was studying in Germany. His mother had visited him in Edinburgh. "I had her," he writes, "at the pier of Leith, and showed her where your ship vanished; and she looked over the blue waters eastward with wettish eyes, and asked the dumb waves 'when he would be back again.' Good mother."

To see more of Ecclefechan and its people, and to browse more at my leisure about the country, I brought my wife and youngster down from Lockerbie; and we spent several days there, putting up at the quiet and cleanly little Bush Inn. I tramped much about the neighborhood, noting the birds, the wild

flowers, the people, the farm occupations, etc.;
going one afternoon to Scotsbrig, where the Carlyles
lived after they left Mainhill, and where both father
and mother died; one day to Annan, another to
Repentance Hill, another over the hill toward Kirtlebridge, tasting the land, and finding it good. It
is an evidence of how permanent and unchanging
things are here that the house where Carlyle was
born, eighty-seven years ago, and which his father
built, stands just as it did then, and looks good for
several hundred years more. In going up to the
little room where he first saw the light, one ascends
the much-worn but original stone stairs, and treads
upon the original stone floors. I suspect that even
the window panes in the little window remain the
same. The village is a very quiet and humble one,
paved with small cobble-stone, over which one hears
the clatter of the wooden clogs, the same as in Carlyle's early days. The pavement comes quite up
to the low, modest, stone-floored houses, and one
steps from the street directly into most of them.
When an Englishman or a Scotchman of the humbler ranks builds a house in the country, he either
turns its back upon the highway, or places it several rods distant from it, with sheds or stables
between; or else he surrounds it with a high, massive fence, shutting out your view entirely. In the
village he crowds it to the front; continues the
street pavement into his hall, if he can; allows no
fence or screen between it and the street, but makes
the communication between the two as easy and

open as possible. At least this is the case with most of the older houses. Hence village houses and cottages in Britain are far less private and secluded than ours, and country houses far less public. The only feature of Ecclefechan, besides the church, that distinguishes it from the humblest peasant village of a hundred years ago, is the large, fine stone structure used for the public school. It confers a sort of distinction upon the place, as if it were in some way connected with the memory of its famous son. I think I was informed that he had some hand in founding it. The building in which he first attended school is a low, humble dwelling, that now stands behind the church, and forms part of the boundary between the cemetery and the Annan road.

From our window I used to watch the laborers on their way to their work, the children going to school, or to the pump for water, and night and morning the women bringing in their cows from the pasture to be milked. In the long June gloaming the evening milking was not done till about nine o'clock. On two occasions, the first in a brisk rain, a bedraggled, forlorn, deeply-hooded, youngish woman, came slowly through the street, pausing here and there, and singing in wild, melancholy, and not unpleasing strains. Her voice had a strange piercing plaintiveness and wildness. Now and then some passer-by would toss a penny at her feet. The pretty Edinburgh lass, her hair redder than Scotch gold, that waited upon us at the inn, went out in the rain and put a penny in her hand. After a few pennies had been collected the music would stop, and the singer disappear, — to drink up her gains, I half suspect, but do not know. I noticed that she was never treated with rudeness or disrespect. The boys would pause and regard her occasionally, but made no remark, or gesture, or grimace. One afternoon a traveling show pitched its tent in the broader part of the street, and by diligent grinding of a hand-organ summoned all the children of the place to see the wonders. The admission was one penny, and I went in with the rest, and saw the little man, the big dog, the happy family, and the gaping, dirty-faced, but orderly crowd of boys and girls. The Ecclefechan boys, with some of whom I tried, not very successfully, to scrape an acquaintance, I found a sober, quiet, modest set, shy of strangers, and, like all country boys, incipient naturalists. If you want to know where the birds'-nests are, ask the boys. Hence, one Sunday afternoon, meeting a couple of them on the Annan road, I put the inquiry. They looked rather blank and unresponsive at first; but I made them understand I was in earnest, and wished to be shown some nests. To stimulate their ornithology I offered a penny for the first nest, twopence for the second, threepence for the third, etc., — a reward that, as it turned out, lightened my burden of British copper considerably; for these boys appeared to know every nest in the neighborhood, and I suspect had just then been making Sunday calls upon their feath-

ered friends. They turned about, with a bashful
smile, but without a word, and marched me a few
paces along the road, when they stepped to the
hedge, and showed me a hedge-sparrow's nest with
young. The mother bird was near, with food in
her beak. This nest is a great favorite of the
cuckoo, and is the one to which Shakespeare refers: —

> " The hedge-sparrow fed the cuckoo so long
> That it 's had it head bit off by it young."

The bird is not a sparrow at all, but is a warbler,
closely related to the nightingale. Then they conducted me along a pretty by-road, and parted away
the branches, and showed me a sparrow's nest with
eggs in it. A group of wild pansies, the first I
had seen, made bright the bank near it. Next,
after conferring a moment soberly together, they
took me to a robin's nest, — a warm, mossy structure in the side of the bank. Then we wheeled
up another road, and they disclosed the nest of the
yellow yite, or yellow-hammer, a bird of the sparrow kind, also upon the ground. It seemed to
have a little platform of coarse, dry stalks, like a
door-stone, in front of it. In the mean time they
had showed me several nests of the hedge-sparrow,
and one of the shilfa, or chaffinch, that had been
"harried," as the boys said, or robbed. These
were gratuitous and merely by the way. Then they
pointed out to me the nest of a tomtit in a disused
pump that stood near the cemetery; after which
they proposed to conduct me to a chaffinch's nest

and a blackbird's nest; but I said I had already seen several of these and my curiosity was satisfied. Did they know any others? Yes, several of them; beyond the village, on the Middlebie road, they knew a wren's nest with eighteen eggs in it. Well, I would see that, and that would be enough; the coppers were changing pockets too fast. So through the village we went, and along the Middlebie road for nearly a mile. The boys were as grave and silent as if they were attending a funeral; not a remark, not a smile. We walked rapidly. The afternoon was warm, for Scotland, and the tips of their ears glowed through their locks, as they wiped their brows. I began to feel as if I had had about enough walking myself. "Boys, how much farther is it?" I said. "A wee bit farther, sir;" and presently, by their increasing pace, I knew we were nearing it. It proved to be the nest of the willow wren, or willow warbler, an exquisite structure, with a dome or canopy above it, the cavity lined with feathers and crowded with eggs. But it did not contain eighteen. The boys said they had been told that the bird would lay as many as eighteen eggs; but it is the common wren that lays this number, — even more. What struck me most was the gravity and silent earnestness of the boys. As we walked back they showed me more nests that had been harried. The elder boy's name was Thomas. He had heard of Thomas Carlyle; but when I asked him what he thought of him, he only looked awkwardly upon the ground.

I had less trouble to get the opinion of an old road-mender whom I fell in with one day. I was walking toward Repentance Hill, when he overtook me with his "machine" (all road vehicles in Scotland are called machines), and insisted upon my getting up beside him. He had a little white pony, "twenty-one years old, sir," and a heavy, rattling two-wheeler, quite as old I should say. We discoursed about roads. Had we good roads in America? No? Had we no "metal" there, no stone? Plenty of it, I told him, — too much; but we had not learned the art of road-making yet. Then he would have to come "out" and show us; indeed, he had been seriously thinking about it; he had an uncle in America, but had lost all track of him. He had seen Carlyle many a time, "but the people here took no interest in that man," he said; "he never done nothing for this place." Referring to Carlyle's ancestors, he said, "The Cairls were what we Scotch call bullies, — a set of bullies, sir. If you crossed their path, they would murder you;" and then came out some highly-colored tradition of the "Ecclefechan dog fight," which Carlyle refers to in his Reminiscences. On this occasion, the old road-mender said, the "Cairls" had clubbed together, and bullied and murdered half the people of the place! "No, sir, we take no interest in that man here," and he gave the pony a sharp punch with his stub of a whip. But he himself took a friendly interest in the schoolgirls whom we overtook along the road, and kept picking them up till the cart was full, and giving the "lassies" a lift on their way home. Beyond Annan bridge we parted company, and a short walk brought me to Repentance Hill, a grassy eminence that commands a wide prospect toward the Solway. The tower which stands on the top is one of those interesting relics of which this land is full, and all memory and tradition of the use and occasion of which are lost. It is a rude stone structure, about thirty feet square and forty high, pierced by a single door, with the word "Repentance" cut in Old English letters in the lintel over it. The walls are loopholed here and there for musketry or archery. An old disused graveyard surrounds it, and the walls of a little chapel stand in the rear of it. The conies have their holes under it; some lord, whose castle lies in the valley below, has his flagstaff upon it; and Time's initials are scrawled on every stone. A piece of mortar probably three or four hundred years old, that had fallen from its place, I picked up, and found nearly as hard as the stone, and quite as gray and lichen-covered. Returning, I stood some time on Annan bridge, looking over the parapet into the clear, swirling water, now and then seeing a trout leap. Whenever the pedestrian comes to one of these arched bridges, he must pause and admire, it is so unlike what he is acquainted with at home. It is a real *viaduct ;* it conducts not merely the traveler over, it conducts the road over as well. Then an arched bridge is ideally perfect; there is no room for criticism, — not one superfluous touch or stroke; every stone tells, and tells

entirely. Of a piece of architecture, we can say
this or that, but of one of these old bridges this
only: it satisfies every sense of the mind. It has
the beauty of poetry, and the precision of mathe-
matics. The older bridges, like this over the Annan, are slightly hipped, so that the road rises
gradually from either side to the key of the arch;
this adds to their beauty, and makes them look
more like things of life. The modern bridges are
all level on the top, which increases their utility.
Two laborers, gossiping on the bridge, said I could
fish by simply going and asking leave of some func-
tionary about the castle.

Shakespeare says of the martlet, that it

> " Builds in the weather on the outward wall,
> Even in the force and road of casualty."

I noticed that a pair had built their nest on an iron
bracket under the eaves of a building opposite our
inn, which proved to be in the "road of casualty;"
for one day the painters began scraping the building, preparatory to giving it a new coat of paint,
and the "procreant cradle" was knocked down.
The swallows did not desert the place, however,
but were at work again next morning before the
painters were. The Scotch, by the way, make a
free use of paint. They even paint their tomb-
stones. Most of them, I observed, were brown
stones painted white. Carlyle's father once sternly
drove the painters from his door when they had
been summoned by the younger members of his
family to give the house a coat "o' pent." "Ye

can jist pent the bog wi' yer ashbaket feet, for ye 'll pit nane o' yer glaur on ma door." But the painters have had their revenge at last, and their "glaur" now covers the old man's tombstone.

One day I visited a little overgrown cemetery about a mile below the village, toward Kirtlebridge, and saw many of the graves of the old stock of Carlyles, among them some of Carlyle's uncles. This name occurs very often in those old cemeteries; they were evidently a prolific and hardy race. The name Thomas is a favorite one among them, insomuch that I saw the graves and headstones of eight Thomas Carlyles in the two graveyards. The oldest Carlyle tomb I saw was that of one John Carlyle, who died in 1692. The inscription upon his stone is as follows: —

"Heir Lyes John Carlyle of Penerssaughs, who departed this life ye 17 of May 1692, and of age 72, and His Spouse Jannet Davidson, who departed this life Febr. ye 7, 1708, and of age 73. Erected by John, his son."

The old sexton, whom I frequently saw in the churchyard, lives in the Carlyle house. He knew the family well, and had some amusing and characteristic anecdotes to relate of Carlyle's father, the redoubtable James, mainly illustrative of his bluntness and plainness of speech. The sexton pointed out, with evident pride, the few noted graves the churchyard held; that of the elder Peel being among them. He spoke of many of the oldest graves as "extinct;" nobody owned or claimed them; the name had disappeared, and the ground was used a second time. The ordinary graves in these old burying places appear to become "extinct" in about two hundred years. It was very rare to find a date older than that. He said the "Cairls" were a peculiar set; there was nobody like them. You would know them, man and woman, as soon as they opened their mouths to speak; they spoke as if against a stone wall. (Their words hit hard.) This is somewhat like Carlyle's own view of his style. "My style," he says in his note-book, when he was thirty-eight years of age, "is like no other man's. The first sentence bewrays me." Indeed, Carlyle's style, which has been so criticised, was as much a part of himself, and as little an affectation, as his shock of coarse yeoman hair and bristly beard and bleared eyes were a part of himself; he inherited them. What Taine calls his barbarisms was his strong mason sire cropping out. He was his father's son to the last drop of his blood, a master builder working with might and main. No more did the former love to put a rock face upon his wall than did the latter to put the same rock face upon his sentences; and he could do it, too, as no other writer, ancient or modern, could.

I occasionally saw strangers at the station, which is a mile from the village, inquiring their way to the churchyard; but I was told there had been a notable falling off of the pilgrims and visitors of late. During the first few months after his burial, they nearly denuded the grave of its turf; but after the publication of the Reminiscences, the number of silly geese that came there to crop the grass was much fewer. No real lover of Carlyle was ever disturbed by those Reminiscences; but to the throng that run after a man because he is famous, and that chip his headstone or carry away the turf above him when he is dead, they were happily a great bugaboo.

A most agreeable walk I took one day down to Annan. Irving's name still exists there, but I believe all his near kindred have disappeared. Across the street from the little house where he was born this sign may be seen: "Edward Irving, Flesher." While in Glasgow, I visited Irving's grave, in the crypt of the cathedral, a most dismal place, and was touched to see the bronze tablet that marked its site in the pavement bright and shining, while those about it, of Sir this or Lady that, were dull and tarnished. Did some devoted hand keep it scoured, or was the polishing done by the many feet that paused thoughtfully above this name? Irving would long since have been forgotten by the world had it not been for his connection with Carlyle, and it was probably the lustre of the latter's memory that I saw reflected in the metal that bore Irving's name. The two men must have been of kindred genius in many ways, to have been so drawn to each other, but Irving had far less hold upon reality; his written word has no projectile force. It makes a vast difference whether you burn gunpowder on a shovel or in a gun-barrel. Irving may be said to have made a brilliant flash, and then to have disappeared in the smoke.

Some men are like nails, easily drawn; others are like rivets, not drawable at all. Carlyle is a rivet, well *headed* in. He is not going to give way, and be forgotten soon. People who differed from him in opinion have stigmatized him as an actor, a mountebank, a rhetorician; but he was committed to his purpose and to the part he played with the force of gravity. Behold how he toiled! He says, "One monster there is in the world, — the idle man." He did not merely preach the gospel of work; he was it, — an indomitable worker from first to last. How he delved! How he searched for a sure foundation, like a master builder, fighting his way through rubbish and quicksands till he reached the rock! Each of his review articles cost him a month or more of serious work. "Sartor Resartus" cost him nine months, the "French Revolution" three years, "Cromwell" four years, "Frederick" thirteen years. No surer does the Auldgarth bridge, that his father helped build, carry the traveler over the turbulent water beneath it, than these books convey the reader over chasms and confusions, where before there was no way, or only an inadequate one. Carlyle never wrote a book except to clear some gulf or quagmire, to span and conquer some chaos. No architect or engineer ever had purpose more tangible and definite. To further the reader on his way, not to beguile or amuse him, was always his purpose. He had that contempt for all dallying and toying and lightness and frivolousness that hard, serious workers always have.

He was impatient of poetry and art; they savored
too much of play and levity. His own work was
not done lightly and easily, but with labor throes
and pains, as of planting his piers in a weltering
flood and chaos. The spirit of struggling and
wrestling which he had inherited was always upper-
most. It seems as if the travail and yearning of his
mother had passed upon him as a birthmark. The
universe was madly rushing about him, seeking to
engulf him. Things assumed threatening and spec-
tral shapes. There was little joy or serenity for
him. Every task he proposed to himself was a
struggle with chaos and darkness, real or imaginary.
He speaks of "Frederick" as a nightmare; the
"Cromwell business" as toiling amid mountains of
dust. I know of no other man in literature with
whom the sense of labor is so tangible and terrible.
That vast, grim, struggling, silent, inarticulate
array of ancestral force that lay in him, when the
burden of written speech was laid upon it, half
rebelled, and would not cease to struggle and be
inarticulate. There was a plethora of power: a
channel, as through rocks, had to be made for it,
and there was an incipient cataclysm whenever a
book was to be written. What brings joy and
buoyancy to other men, namely, a genial task,
brought despair and convulsions to him. It is not
the effort of composition, — he was a rapid and
copious writer and speaker, — but the pressure of
purpose, the friction of power and velocity, the
sense of overcoming the demons and mud-gods and

frozen torpidity he so often refers to. Hence no
writing extant is so little like writing, and gives
so vividly the sense of something *done*. He may
praise silence and glorify work. The unspeakable
is ever present with him: it is the core of every
sentence: the inarticulate is round about him; a
solitude like that of space encompasseth him. His
books are not easy reading; they are a kind of
wrestling to most persons. His style is like a road
made of rocks: when it is good, there is nothing
like it; and when it is bad, there is nothing like it!

In "Past and Present" Carlyle has unconsciously
painted his own life and character in truer colors
than has any one else: "Not a May-game is this
man's life, but a battle and a march, a warfare with
principalities and powers; no idle promenade through
fragrant orange groves and green, flowery spaces,
waited on by the choral Muses and the rosy Hours:
it is a stern pilgrimage through burning, sandy
solitudes, through regions of thick-ribbed ice. He
walks among men; loves men with inexpressible
soft pity, as they *cannot* love him: but his soul
dwells in solitude, in the uttermost parts of Creation. In green oases by the palm-tree wells, he
rests a space; but anon he has to journey forward,
escorted by the Terrors and the Splendors, the
Archdemons and Archangels. All heaven, all pandemonium, are his escort." Part of the world will
doubtless persist in thinking that pandemonium furnished his chief counsel and guide; but there are
enough who think otherwise, and their numbers are
bound to increase in the future.

IV

A HUNT FOR THE NIGHTINGALE

WHILE I lingered away the latter half of May in Scotland, and the first half of June in northern England, and finally in London, intent on seeing the land leisurely and as the mood suited, the thought never occurred to me that I was in danger of missing one of the chief pleasures I had promised myself in crossing the Atlantic, namely, the hearing of the song of the nightingale. Hence, when on the 17th of June I found myself down among the copses near Hazlemere, on the borders of Surrey and Sussex, and was told by the old farmer, to whose house I had been recommended by friends in London, that I was too late, that the season of the nightingale was over, I was a good deal disturbed.

"I think she be done singing now, sir; I ain't heered her in some time, sir," said my farmer, as we sat down to get acquainted over a mug of the hardest cider I ever attempted to drink.

"Too late!" I said in deep chagrin, "and I might have been here weeks ago."

"Yeas, sir, she be done now; May is the time to hear her. The cuckoo is done too, sir; and you

don't hear the nightingale after the cuckoo is gone,
sir."

(The country people in this part of England *sir*
one at the end of every sentence, and talk with an
indescribable drawl.)

But I had heard a cuckoo that very afternoon,
and I took heart from the fact. I afterward learned
that the country people everywhere associate these
two birds in this way; you will not hear the one
after the other has ceased. But I heard the cuckoo
almost daily till the middle of July. Matthew
Arnold reflects the popular opinion when in one of
his poems ("Thyrsis") he makes the cuckoo say in
early June, —

> "The bloom is gone, and with the bloom go I !"

The explanation is to be found in Shakespeare, who
says, —

> "The cuckoo is in June
> Heard, not regarded,"

as the bird really does not go till August. I got
out my Gilbert White, as I should have done at an
earlier day, and was still more disturbed to find
that he limited the singing of the nightingale to
June 15. But seasons differ, I thought, and it
can't be possible that any class of feathered songsters all stop on a given day. There is a tradition
that when George I. died the nightingales all ceased
singing for the year out of grief at the sad event;
but his majesty did not die till June 21. This
would give me a margin of several days. Then,
when I looked further in White, and found that he

says the chaffinch ceases to sing the beginning of
June, I took more courage, for I had that day heard
the chaffinch also. But it was evident I had no
time to lose; I was just on the dividing line, and
any day might witness the cessation of the last
songster. For it seems that the nightingale ceases
singing the moment her brood is hatched. After
that event, you hear only a harsh chiding or anxious
note. Hence the poets, who attribute her melancholy strains to sorrow for the loss of her young,
are entirely at fault. Virgil, portraying the grief
of Orpheus after the loss of Eurydice, says: —

> " So Philomela, 'mid the poplar shade,
> Bemoans her captive brood; the cruel hind
> Saw them unplumed, and took them; but all night
> Grieves she, and, sitting on a bough, runs o'er
> Her wretched tale, and fills the woods with woe."

But she probably does nothing of the kind. The
song of a bird is not a reminiscence, but an antici-
pation, and expresses happiness or joy only, except
in those cases where the male bird, having lost its
mate, sings for a few days as if to call the lost one
back. When the male renews his powers of song,
after the young brood has been destroyed, or after
it has flown away, it is a sign that a new brood is
contemplated. The song is, as it were, the magic
note that calls the brood forth. At least, this is
the habit with other song-birds, and I have no
doubt the same holds good with the nightingale.
Destroy the nest or brood of the wood thrush, and
if the season is not too far advanced, after a week

or ten days of silence, during which the parent
birds by their manner seem to bemoan their loss
and to take counsel together, the male breaks forth
with a new song, and the female begins to construct
a new nest. The poets, therefore, in depicting the
bird on such occasions as bewailing the lost brood,
are wide of the mark; he is invoking and celebrat-
ing a new brood.

As it was mid-afternoon, I could only compose
myself till nightfall. I accompanied the farmer to
the hay-field and saw the working of his mowing-
machine, a rare implement in England, as most of
the grass is still cut by hand, and raked by hand
also. The disturbed skylarks were hovering above
the falling grass, full of anxiety for their nests, as
one may note the bobolinks on like occasions at
home. The weather is so uncertain in England,
and it is so impossible to predict its complexion,
not only from day to day but from hour to hour,
that the farmers appear to consider it a suitable time
to cut grass when it is not actually raining. They
slash away without reference to the aspects of the
sky, and when the field is down trust to luck to be
able to cure the hay, or get it ready to "carry"
between the showers. The clouds were lowering
and the air was damp now, and it was Saturday
afternoon; but the farmer said they would never
get their hay if they minded such things. The
farm had seen better days; so had the farmer; both
were slightly down at the heel. Too high rent and
too much hard cider were working their effects upon

both. The farm had been in the family many generations, but it was now about to be sold and to
pass into other hands, and my host said he was glad
of it. There was no money in farming any more;
no money in anything. I asked him what were
the main sources of profit on such a farm.

"Well," he said, "sometimes the wheat pops up,
and the barley drops in, and the pigs come on, and
we picks up a little money, sir, but not much, sir.
Pigs is doing well naow. But they brings so much
wheat from Ameriky, and our weather is so bad
that we can't get a good sample, sir, one year in
three, that there is no money made in growing
wheat, sir." And the "wuts" (oats) were not
much better. "Theys as would buy hain't got no
money, sir." "Up to the top of the nip," for top
of the hill, was one of his expressions. Tennyson
had a summer residence at Blackdown, not far off.
"One of the Queen's poets, I believe, sir." "Yes,
I often see him riding about, sir."

After an hour or two with the farmer, I walked
out to take a survey of the surrounding country.
It was quite wild and irregular, full of bushy fields
and overgrown hedge-rows, and looked to me very
nightingaly. I followed for a mile or two a road
that led by tangled groves and woods and copses,
with a still meadow trout stream in the gentle
valley below. I inquired for nightingales of every
boy and laboring-man I met or saw. I got but
little encouragement; it was too late. "She be
about done singing now, sir." A boy whom I met

in a footpath that ran through a pasture beside a
copse said, after reflecting a moment, that he had
heard one in that very copse two mornings before,
— "about seven o'clock, sir, while I was on my
way to my work, sir." Then I would try my luck
in said copse and in the adjoining thickets that
night and the next morning. The railway ran
near, but perhaps that might serve to keep the birds
awake. These copses in this part of England look
strange enough to American eyes. What thriftless
farming! the first thought is; behold the fields
grown up to bushes, as if the land had relapsed to
a state of nature again. Adjoining meadows and
grain-fields, one may see an inclosure of many acres
covered with a thick growth of oak and chestnut
sprouts, six or eight or twelve feet high. These
are the copses one has so often heard about, and
they are a valuable and productive part of the farm.
They are planted and preserved as carefully as we
plant an orchard or a vineyard. Once in so many
years, perhaps five or six, the copse is cut and
every twig is saved; it is a woodland harvest that
in our own country is gathered in the forest itself.
The larger poles are tied up in bundles and sold
for hoop-poles; the fine branches and shoots are
made into brooms in the neighboring cottages and
hamlets, or used as material for thatching. The
refuse is used as wood.

About eight o'clock in the evening I sallied
forth, taking my way over the ground I had
explored a few hours before. The gloaming, which

at this season lasts till after ten o'clock, dragged its slow length along. Nine o'clock came, and, though my ear was attuned, the songster was tardy. I hovered about the copses and hedge-rows like one meditating some dark deed; I lingered in a grove and about an overgrown garden and a neglected orchard; I sat on stiles and leaned on wickets, mentally speeding the darkness that should bring my singer out. The weather was damp and chilly, and the tryst grew tiresome. I had brought a rubber water-proof, but not an overcoat. Lining the back of the rubber with a newspaper, I wrapped it about me and sat down, determined to lay siege to my bird. A footpath that ran along the fields and bushes on the other side of the little valley showed every few minutes a woman or girl, or boy or laborer, passing along it. A path near me also had its frequent figures moving along in the dusk. In this country people travel in footpaths as much as in highways. The paths give a private, human touch to the landscape that the roads do not. They are sacred to the human foot. They have the sentiment of domesticity, and suggest the way to cottage doors and to simple, primitive times.

Presently a man with a fishing-rod, and capped, coated, and booted for the work, came through the meadow, and began casting for trout in the stream below me. How he gave himself to the work! how oblivious he was of everything but the one matter in hand! I doubt if he was conscious of the train that passed within a few rods of him.

Your born angler is like a hound that scents no game but that which he is in pursuit of. Every sense and faculty were concentrated upon that hovering fly. This man wooed the stream, quivering with pleasure and expectation. Every foot of it he tickled with his decoy. His close was evidently a short one, and he made the most of it. He lingered over every cast, and repeated it again and again. An American angler would have been out of sight down stream long ago. But this fisherman was not going to bolt his preserve; his line should taste every drop of it. His eager, stealthy movements denoted his enjoyment and his absorption. When a trout was caught, it was quickly rapped on the head and slipped into his basket, as if in punishment for its tardiness in jumping. "Be quicker next time, will you?" (British trout, by the way, are not so beautiful as our own. They have more of a domesticated look. They are less brilliantly marked, and have much coarser scales. There is no gold or vermilion in their coloring.)

Presently there arose from a bushy corner of a near field a low, peculiar purring or humming sound, that sent a thrill through me; of course, I thought my bird was inflating her throat. Then the sound increased, and was answered or repeated in various other directions. It had a curious ventriloquial effect. I presently knew it to be the nightjar or goatsucker, a bird that answers to our whip-poor-will. Very soon the sound seemed to be floating all about me, — *Jr-r-r-r-r* or *Chr-r-r-r-r,* slightly suggesting the call of our toads, but more vague as to direction. Then as it grew darker the birds ceased; the fisherman reeled up and left. No sound was now heard, — not even the voice of a solitary frog anywhere. I never heard a frog in England. About eleven o'clock I moved down by a wood, and stood for an hour on a bridge over the railroad. No voice of bird greeted me till the sedge-warbler struck up her curious nocturne in a hedge near by. It was a singular medley of notes, hurried chirps, trills, calls, warbles, snatched from the songs of other birds, with a half-chiding, remonstrating tone or air running through it all. As there was no other sound to be heard, and as the darkness was complete, it had the effect of a very private and whimsical performance, — as if the little bird had secluded herself there, and was giving vent to her emotions in the most copious and vehement manner. I listened till after midnight, and till the rain began to fall, and the vivacious warbler never ceased for a moment. White says that, if it stops, a stone tossed into the bush near it will set it going again. Its voice is not musical; the quality of it is like that of the loquacious English house sparrows; but its song or medley is so persistently animated, and in such contrast to the gloom and the darkness, that the effect is decidedly pleasing.

This and the nightjar were the only nightingales I heard that night. I returned home, a good deal disappointed, but slept upon my arms, as it were, and was out upon the chase again at four o'clock in the morning. This time I passed down a lane by the neglected garden and orchard, where I was told the birds had sung for weeks past; then under the railroad by a cluster of laborers' cottages, and along a road with many copses and bushy fence-corners on either hand, for two miles, but I heard no nightingales. A boy of whom I inquired seemed half frightened, and went into the house without answering.

After a late breakfast I sallied out again, going farther in the same direction, and was overtaken by several showers. I heard many and frequent bird-songs, — the lark, the wren, the thrush, the black-bird, the whitethroat, the greenfinch, and the hoarse, guttural cooing of the wood-pigeons, — but not the note I was in quest of. I passed up a road that was a deep trench in the side of a hill over-grown with low beeches. The roots of the trees formed a network on the side of the bank, as their branches did above. In a framework of roots, within reach of my hand, I spied a wren's nest a round hole leading to the interior of a large mass of soft green moss, a structure displaying the taste and neatness of the daintiest of bird architects, and the depth and warmth and snugness of the most ingenious mouse habitation. While lingering here, a young countryman came along whom I engaged in conversation. No, he had not heard the night-ingale for a few days; but the previous week he had been in camp with the militia near Guildford

and while on picket duty had heard her nearly all
night. "'Don't she sing splendid to-night?' the
boys would say." This was tantalizing; Guildford
was within easy reach; but the previous week, —
that could not be reached. However, he encouraged me by saying he did not think they were done
singing yet, as he had often heard them during
haying-time. I inquired for the blackcap, but saw
he did not know this bird, and thought I referred
to a species of tomtit, which also has a black cap.
The woodlark I was also on the lookout for, but
he did not know this bird either, and during my
various rambles in England I found but one person
who did. In Scotland it was confounded with the
titlark or pipit.

I next met a man and boy, a villager with a
stove-pipe hat on, — and, as it turned out, a man
of many trades, tailor, barber, painter, etc., — from
Hazlemere. The absorbing inquiry was put to him
also. No, not that day, but a few mornings before
he had. But he could easily call one out, if there
were any about, as he could imitate them. Plucking a spear of grass, he adjusted it behind his teeth
and startled me with the shrill, rapid notes he
poured forth. I at once recognized its resemblance
to the descriptions I had read of the opening part
of the nightingale song, — what is called the
"challenge." The boy said, and he himself
averred, that it was an exact imitation. The *chew,
chew, chew,* and some other parts, were very bird-
like, and I had no doubt were correct. I was

astonished at the strong, piercing quality of the strain. It echoed in the woods and copses about, but, though oft repeated, brought forth no response. With this man I made an engagement to take a walk that evening at eight o'clock along a certain route where he had heard plenty of nightingales but a few days before. He was confident he could call them out; so was I.

In the afternoon, which had gleams of warm sunshine, I made another excursion, less in hopes of hearing my bird than of finding some one who could direct me to the right spot. Once I thought the game was very near. I met a boy who told me he had heard a nightingale only fifteen minutes before, "on Polecat Hill, sir, just this side the Devil's Punch-bowl, sir!" I had heard of his majesty's punch-bowl before, and of the gibbets near it where three murderers were executed nearly a hundred years ago, but Polecat Hill was a new name to me. The combination did not seem a likely place for nightingales, but I walked rapidly thitherward; I heard several warblers, but not Philomel, and was forced to conclude that probably I had crossed the sea to miss my bird by just fifteen minutes. I met many other boys (is there any country where boys do not prowl about in small bands of a Sunday?) and advertised the object of my search freely among them, offering a reward that made their eyes glisten for the bird in song; but nothing ever came of it. In my desperation, I even presented a letter I had brought to the village squire, just as, in company with his wife, he was about to leave his door for church. He turned back, and, hearing my quest, volunteered to take me on a long walk through the wet grass and bushes of his fields and copses, where he knew the birds were wont to sing. "Too late," he said, and so it did appear. He showed me a fine old edition of White's "Selborne," with notes by some editor whose name I have forgotten. This editor had extended White's date of June 15 to July 1, as the time to which the nightingale continues in song, and I felt like thanking him for it, as it gave me renewed hope. The squire thought there was a chance yet; and in case my man with the spear of grass behind his teeth failed me, he gave me a card to an old naturalist and taxidermist at Godalming, a town nine miles above, who, he felt sure, could put me on the right track if anybody could.

At eight o'clock, the sun yet some distance above the horizon, I was at the door of the barber in Hazlemere. He led the way along one of those delightful footpaths with which this country is threaded, extending to a neighboring village several miles distant. It left the street at Hazlemere, cutting through the houses diagonally, as if the brick walls had made way for it, passed between gardens, through wickets, over stiles, across the highway and railroad, through cultivated fields and a gentleman's park, and on toward its destination, — a broad, well-kept path, that seemed to have the same inevitable right of way as a brook. I was told that it was repaired and looked after the same as the highway. Indeed, it was a public way, public to pedestrians only, and no man could stop or turn it aside. We followed it along the side of a steep hill, with copses and groves sweeping down into the valley below us. It was as wild and picturesque a spot as I had seen in England. The foxglove pierced the lower foliage and wild growths everywhere with its tall spires of purple flowers; the wild honeysuckle, with a ranker and coarser fragrance than our cultivated species, was just opening along the hedges. We paused here, and my guide blew his shrill call; he blew it again and again. How it awoke the echoes, and how it awoke all the other songsters! The valley below us and the slope beyond, which before were silent, were soon musical. The chaffinch, the robin, the blackbird, the thrush — the last the loudest and most copious — seemed to vie with each other and with the loud whistler above them. But we listened in vain for the nightingale's note. Twice my guide struck an attitude and said, impressively, "There! I believe I 'erd 'er." But we were obliged to give it up. A shower came on, and after it had passed we moved to another part of the landscape and repeated our call, but got no response, and as darkness set in we returned to the village.

The situation began to look serious. I knew there was a nightingale somewhere whose brood had been delayed from some cause or other, and who was therefore still in song, but I could not get a

clew to the spot. I renewed the search late that
night, and again the next morning; I inquired of
every man and boy I saw.

> "I met many travelers,
>   Who the road had surely kept;
> They saw not my fine revelers, —
>   These had crossed them while they slept;
> Some had heard their fair report,
> In the country or the court."

I soon learned to distrust young fellows and their
girls who had heard nightingales in the gloaming.
I knew one's ears could not always be depended
upon on such occasions, nor his eyes either. Larks
are seen in buntings, and a wren's song entrances
like Philomel's. A young couple of whom I inquired in the train, on my way to Godalming, said
Yes, they had heard nightingales just a few moments before on their way to the station, and
described the spot, so I could find it if I returned
that way. They left the train at the same point I
did, and walked up the street in advance of me. I
had lost sight of them till they beckoned to me
from the corner of the street, near the church,
where the prospect opens with a view of a near
meadow and a stream shaded by pollard willows.
"We heard one now, just there," they said, as I
came up. They passed on, and I bent my ear
eagerly in the direction. Then I walked farther
on, following one of those inevitable footpaths to
where it cuts diagonally through the cemetery
behind the old church, but I heard nothing save a
few notes of the thrush. My ear was too critical

and exacting. Then I sought out the old naturalist
and taxidermist to whom I had a card from the
squire. He was a short, stout man, racy both in
look and speech, and kindly. He had a fine collection of birds and animals, in which he took great
pride. He pointed out the woodlark and the blackcap to me, and told me where he had seen and
heard them. He said I was too late for the nightingale, though I might possibly find one yet in
song. But he said she grew hoarse late in the
season, and did not sing as a few weeks earlier.
He thought our cardinal grosbeak, which he called
the Virginia nightingale, as fine a whistler as the
nightingale herself. He could not go with me that
day, but he would send his boy. Summoning the
lad, he gave him minute directions where to take
me, — over by Easing, around by Shackerford
church, etc., a circuit of four or five miles. Leaving the picturesque old town, we took a road over a
broad, gentle hill, lined with great trees, — beeches,
elms, oaks, — with rich cultivated fields beyond.
The air of peaceful and prosperous human occupancy which everywhere pervades this land seemed
especially pronounced through all this section. The
sentiment of parks and lawns, easy, large, basking,
indifferent of admiration, self-sufficing, and full,
everywhere prevailed. The road was like the most
perfect private carriage-way. Homeliness, in its
true sense, is a word that applies to nearly all English country scenes; homelike, redolent of affectionate care and toil, saturated with rural and domestic

contentment; beauty without pride, order without stiffness, age without decay. This people love the country, because it would seem as if the country must first have loved them. In a field I saw for the first time a new species of clover, much grown in parts of England as green fodder for horses. The farmers call it trifolium, probably *Trifolium incarnatum*. The head is two or three inches long, and as red as blood. A field of it under the sunlight presents a most brilliant appearance. As we walked along, I got also my first view of the British blue jay, — a slightly larger bird than ours, with a hoarser voice and much duller plumage. Blue, the tint of the sky, is not so common, and is not found in any such perfection among the British birds as among the American. My boy companion was worthy of observation also. He was a curiour specimen, ready and officious, but, as one soon found out, full of duplicity. I questioned him about himself. "I helps he, sir; sometimes I shows people about, and sometimes I does errands. I gets three a week, sir, and lunch and tea. I lives with my grandmother, but I calls her mother, sir. The master and the rector they gives me a character, says I am a good, honest boy, and that it is well I went to school in my youth. I am ten, sir. Last year I had the measles, sir, and I thought I should die; but I got hold of a bottle of medicine, and it tasted like honey, and I takes the whole of it, and it made me well, sir. I never lies, sir. It is good to tell the truth." And yet he would slide off into a lie as if the track in that direction was always greased. Indeed, there was a kind of fluent, unctuous, obsequious effrontery in all he said and did. As the day was warm for that climate, he soon grew tired of the chase. At one point we skirted the grounds of a large house, as thickly planted with trees and shrubs as a forest; many birds were singing there, and for a moment my guide made me believe that among them he recognized the notes of the nightingale. Failing in this, he coolly assured me that the swallow that skimmed along the road in front of us was the night-ingale! We presently left the highway and took a footpath. It led along the margin of a large plowed field, shut in by rows of noble trees, the soil of which looked as if it might have been a garden of untold generations. Then the path led through a wicket, and down the side of a wooded hill to a large stream and to the hamlet of Easing. A boy fishing said indifferently that he had heard nightingales there that morning. He had caught a little fish which he said was a gudgeon. "Yes," said my companion in response to a remark of mine, "they's little; but you can eat they if they *is* little." Then we went toward Shackerford church. The road, like most roads in the south of England, was a deep trench. The banks on either side rose fifteen feet, covered with ivy, moss, wild flowers, and the roots of trees. England's best defense against an invading foe is her sunken roads. Whole armies might be ambushed in these trenches, while

an enemy moving across the open plain would very
often find himself plunging headlong into these
hidden pitfalls. Indeed, between the subterranean
character of the roads in some places and the high-
walled or high-hedged character of it in others, the
pedestrian about England is shut out from much he
would like to see. I used to envy the bicyclists,
perched high upon their rolling stilts. But the
footpaths escape the barriers, and one need walk
nowhere else if he choose.

Around Shackerford church are copses, and large
pine and fir woods. The place was full of birds.
My guide threw a stone at a small bird which he
declared was a nightingale; and though the missile
did not come within three yards of it, yet he said
he had hit it, and pretended to search for it on the
ground. He must needs invent an opportunity for
lying. I told him here I had no further use for
him, and he turned cheerfully back, with my shilling in his pocket. I spent the afternoon about the
woods and copses near Shackerford. The day was
bright and the air balmy. I heard the cuckoo call,
and the chaffinch sing, both of which I considered
good omens. The little chiffchaff was chiffchaffing
in the pine woods. The whitethroat, with his
quick, emphatic *Chew-che-rick* or *Che-rick-a-rew*,
flitted and ducked and hid among the low bushes
by the roadside. A girl told me she had heard the
nightingale yesterday on her way to Sunday-school,
and pointed out the spot. It was in some bushes
near a house. I hovered about this place till I

was afraid the woman, who saw me from the window, would think I had some designs upon her premises. But I managed to look very indifferent or abstracted when I passed. I am quite sure I heard the chiding, guttural note of the bird I was after. Doubtless her brood had come out that very day. Another girl had heard a nightingale on her way to school that morning, and directed me to the road; still another pointed out to me the white-throat and said that was my bird. This last was a rude shock to my faith in the ornithology of schoolgirls. Finally, I found a laborer breaking stone by the roadside, — a serious, honest-faced man, who said he had heard my bird that morning on his way to work; he heard her every morning, and nearly every night, too. He heard her last night after the shower (just at the hour when my barber and I were trying to awaken her near Hazle-mere), and she sang as finely as ever she did. This was a great lift. I felt that I could trust this man. He said that after his day's work was done, that is, at five o'clock, if I chose to accompany him on his way home, he would show me where he had heard the bird. This I gladly agreed to; and, remembering that I had had no dinner, I sought out the inn in the village and asked for something to eat. The unwonted request so startled the landlord that he came out from behind his inclosed bar and confronted me with good-humored curiosity. These back-country English inns, as I several times found to my discomfiture, are only drinking places

for the accommodation of local customers, mainly
of the laboring class.   Instead of standing conspic-
uously on some street corner, as with us, they
usually stand on some byway, or some little paved
court away from the main thoroughfare.   I could
have plenty of beer, said the landlord, but he had
not a mouthful of meat in the house.   I urged my
needs, and finally got some rye-bread and cheese.
With this and a glass of home-brewed beer I was
fairly well fortified.   At the appointed time I met
the cottager and went with him on his way home.
We walked two miles or more along a charming
road, full of wooded nooks and arbor-like vistas.
Why do English trees always look so sturdy, and
exhibit such massive repose, so unlike, in this
latter respect, to the nervous and agitated expression of most of our own foliage?   Probably because
they have been a long time out of the woods, and
have had plenty of room in which to develop individual traits and peculiarities; then, in a deep fertile soil, and a climate that does not hurry or over-
tax, they grow slow and last long, and come to
have the picturesqueness of age without its infirmi-
ties.   The oak, the elm, the beech, all have more
striking profiles than in our country.

   Presently my companion pointed out to me a
small wood below the road that had a wide fringe
of bushes and saplings connecting it with a meadow,
amid which stood the tree-embowered house of a
city man, where he had heard the nightingale in
the morning; and then, farther along, showed me,

near his own cottage, where he had heard one the evening before. It was now only six o'clock, and I had two or three hours to wait before I could reasonably expect to hear her. "It gets to be into the hevening," said my new friend, "when she sings the most, you know." I whiled away the time as best I could. If I had been an artist, I should have brought away a sketch of a picturesque old cottage near by, that bore the date of 1688 on its wall. I was obliged to keep moving most of the time to keep warm. Yet the "no-see-'ems," or midges, annoyed me, in a temperature which at home would have chilled them buzzless and biteless. Finally, I leaped the smooth masonry of the stone wall and ambushed myself amid the tall ferns under a pine-tree, where the nightingale had been heard in the morning. If the keeper had seen me, he would probably have taken me for a poacher. I sat shivering there till nine o'clock, listening to the cooing of the wood-pigeons, watching the motions of a jay that, I suspect, had a nest near by, and taking note of various other birds. The song-thrush and the robins soon made such a musical uproar along the borders of a grove, across an adjoining field, as quite put me out. It might veil and obscure the one voice I wanted to hear. The robin continued to sing quite into the darkness. This bird is related to the nightingale, and looks and acts like it at a little distance; and some of its notes are remarkably piercing and musical. When my patience was about exhausted, I was startled by

a quick, brilliant call or whistle, a few rods from
me, that at once recalled my barber with his blade
of grass, and I knew my long-sought bird was inflating her throat. How it woke me up! It had
the quality that startles; it pierced the gathering
gloom like a rocket. Then it ceased. Suspecting
I was too near the singer, I moved away cautiously,
and stood in a lane beside the wood, where a loping
hare regarded me a few paces away. Then my
singer struck up again, but I could see did not let
herself out; just tuning her instrument, I thought,
and getting ready to transfix the silence and the
darkness. A little later, a man and boy came up
the lane. I asked them if that was the nightingale
singing; they listened, and assured me it was none
other. "Now she's on, sir; now she's on. Ah!
but she don't stick. In May, sir, they makes the
woods all heccho about here. Now she's on again;
that's her, sir; now she's off; she won't stick."
And stick she would not. I could hear a hoarse
wheezing and clucking sound beneath her notes,
when I listened intently. The man and boy moved
away. I stood mutely invoking all the gentle
divinities to spur the bird on. Just then a bird
like our hermit thrush came quickly over the hedge
a few yards below me, swept close past my face,
and back into the thicket. I had been caught listening; the offended bird had found me taking
notes of her dry and worn-out pipe there behind
the hedge, and the concert abruptly ended; not
another note; not a whisper. I waited a long time

and then moved off; then came back, implored
the outraged bird to resume; then rushed off, and
slammed the door, or rather the gate, indignantly
behind me. I paused by other shrines, but not a
sound. The cottager had told me of a little village
three miles beyond, where there were three inns,
and where I could probably get lodgings for the
night. I walked rapidly in that direction; committed myself to a footpath; lost the trail, and
brought up at a little cottage in a wide expanse of
field or common, and by the good woman, with a
babe in her arms, was set right again. I soon
struck the highway by the bridge, as I had been
told, and a few paces brought me to the first inn.
It was ten o'clock, and the lights were just about
to be put out, as the law or custom is in country
inns. The landlady said she could not give me a
bed ; she had only one spare room, and that was not
in order, and she should not set about putting it in
shape at that hour; and she was short and sharp
about it, too. I hastened on to the next one.
The landlady said she had no sheets, and the bed
was damp and unfit to sleep in. I protested that
I thought an inn was an inn, and for the accommodation of travelers. But she referred me to the
next house. Here were more people, and more the
look and air of a public house. But the wife (the
man does not show himself on such occasions) said
her daughter had just got married and come home,
and she had much company and could not keep me.
In vain I urged my extremity; there was no room.

Could I have something to eat, then? This seemed doubtful, and led to consultations in the kitchen; but, finally, some bread and cold meat were produced. The nearest hotel was Godalming, seven miles distant, and I knew all the inns would be shut up before I could get there. So I munched my bread and meat, consoling myself with the thought that perhaps this was just the ill wind that would blow me the good I was in quest of. I saw no alternative but to spend a night under the trees with the nightingales; and I might surprise them at their revels in the small hours of the morning. Just as I was ready to congratulate myself on the richness of my experience, the landlady came in and said there was a young man there going with a "trap" to Godalming, and he had offered to take me in. I feared I should pass for an escaped lunatic if I declined the offer; so I reluctantly assented, and we were presently whirling through the darkness, along a smooth, winding road, toward town. The young man was a drummer; was from Lincolnshire, and said I spoke like a Lincolnshire man. I could believe it, for I told him he talked more like an American than any native I had met. The hotels in the larger towns close at eleven, and I was set down in front of one just as the clock was striking that hour. I asked to be conducted to a room at once. As I was about getting in bed there was a rap at the door, and a waiter presented me my bill on a tray. "Gentlemen as have no luggage, etc." he explained; and pretend to be looking for nightingales, too! Three-and-sixpence; two shillings for the bed and one-and-six for service. I was out at five in the morning, before any one inside was astir. After much trying of bars and doors, I made my exit into a paved court, from which a covered way led into the street. A man opened a window and directed me how to undo the great door, and forth I started, still hoping to catch my bird at her matins. I took the route of the day before. On the edge of the beautiful plowed field, looking down through the trees and bushes into the gleam of the river twenty rods below, I was arrested by the note I longed to hear. It came up from near the water, and made my ears tingle. I folded up my rubber coat and sat down upon it, saying, Now we will take our fill. But — the bird ceased, and, tarry though I did for an hour, not another note reached me. The prize seemed destined to elude me each time just as I thought it mine. Still, I treasured what little I had heard.

It was enough to convince me of the superior quality of the song, and make me more desirous than ever to hear the complete strain. I continued my rambles, and in the early morning once more hung about the Shackerford copses and loitered along the highways. Two schoolboys pointed out a tree to me in which they had heard the nightingale, on their way for milk, two hours before. But I could only repeat Emerson's lines: —

> "Right good-will my sinews strung,
> But no speed of mine avails
> To hunt up their shining trails."

At nine o'clock I gave over the pursuit and returned to Easing in quest of breakfast. Bringing up in front of the large and comfortable-looking inn, I found the mistress of the house with her daughter engaged in washing windows. Perched upon their step-ladders, they treated my request for breakfast very coldly; in fact, finally refused to listen to it at all. The fires were out, and I could not be served. So I must continue my walk back to Goldalming; and, in doing so, I found that one may walk three miles on indignation quite as easily as upon bread.

In the afternoon I returned to my lodgings at Shotter Mill, and made ready for a walk to Selborne, twelve miles distant, part of the way to be accomplished that night in the gloaming, and the rest early on the following morning, to give the nightingales a chance to make any reparation they might feel inclined to for the neglect with which they had treated me. There was a footpath over the hill and through Leechmere bottom to Liphook, and to this, with the sun half an hour high, I committed myself. The feature in this hill scenery of Surrey and Sussex that is new to American eyes is given by the furze and heather, broad black or dark-brown patches of which sweep over the high rolling surfaces, like sable mantles. Tennyson's house stands amid this dusky scenery, a few miles east of Hazlemere. The path led through a large common, partly covered with grass and partly grown up to furze, — another un-American feature.

Doubly precious is land in England, and yet so
much of it given to parks and pleasure-grounds, and
so much of it left unreclaimed in commons! These
commons are frequently met with; about Selborne
they are miles in extent, and embrace the Hanger
and other woods. No one can inclose them, or
appropriate them to his own use. The landed pro-
prietor of whose estates they form a part cannot;
they belong to the people, to the lease-holders.
The villagers and others who own houses on leased
and pasture their cows upon them, gather the
urze, and cut the wood. In some places the commons belong to the crown and are crown lands.
These large uninclosed spaces often give a free-and-
easy air to the landscape that is very welcome.
Near the top of the hill I met a little old man
nearly hidden beneath a burden of furze. He was
backing it home for fuel and other uses. He
paused obsequious, and listened to my inquiries.
A dwarfish sort of man, whose ugliness was redolent of the humblest chimney corner. Bent beneath
his bulky burden, and grinning upon me, he was
a visible embodiment of the poverty, ignorance, and,
I may say, the domesticity of the lowliest peasant
home. I felt as if I had encountered a walking
superstition, fostered beside a hearth lighted by
furze fagots and by branches dropped by the nest-
ing rooks and ravens, — a figure half repulsive and
half alluring. On the border of Leechmere bottom
I sat down above a straggling copse, aflame as usual
with the foxglove, and gave eye and ear to the

scene. While sitting here, I saw and heard for the first time the black-capped warbler. I recognized the note at once by its brightness and strength, and a faint suggestion in it of the nightingale's. But it was disappointing: I had expected a nearer approach to its great rival. The bird was very shy, but did finally show herself fairly several times, as she did also near Selborne, where I heard the song oft repeated and prolonged. It is a ringing, animated strain, but as a whole seemed to me crude, not smoothly and finely modulated. I could name several of our own birds that surpass it in pure music. Like its congeners, the garden warbler and the whitethroat, it sings with great emphasis and strength, but its song is silvern, not golden. "Little birds with big voices," one says to himself after having heard most of the British songsters. My path led me an adventurous course through the copses and bottoms and open commons, in the long twilight. At one point I came upon three young men standing together and watching a dog that was working a near field, — one of them probably the squire's son, and the other two habited like laborers. In a little thicket near by there was a brilliant chorus of bird voices, the robin, the song-thrush, and the blackbird, all vying with each other. To my inquiry, put to test the reliability of the young countrymen's ears, they replied that one of the birds I heard was the nightingale, and, after a moment's attention, singled out the robin as the bird in question. This incident so impressed

me that I paid little attention to the report of the
next man I met, who said he had heard a nightingale just around a bend in the road, a few minutes'
walk in advance of me.   At ten o'clock I reached
Liphook.   I expected and half hoped the inn would
turn its back upon me again, in which case I proposed to make for Wolmer Forest, a few miles distant, but it did not.   Before going to bed, I took
a short and hasty walk down a promising-looking
lane, and again met a couple who had heard nightingales.   "It was a nightingale, was it not, Char-
ley ? "

If all the people of whom I inquired for nightingales in England could have been together and
compared notes, they probably would not have been
long in deciding that there was at least one crazy
American abroad.

I proposed to be up and off at five o'clock in the
morning, which seemed greatly to puzzle mine host.
At first he thought it could not be done, but finally
saw his way out of the dilemma, and said he would
get up and undo the door for me himself.   The
morning was cloudy and misty, though the previous
night had been of the fairest.   There is one thing
they do not have in England that we can boast of
at home, and that is a good masculine type of
weather: it is not even feminine; it is childish and
puerile, though I am told that occasionally there is
a full-grown storm.   But I saw nothing but petu-
lant little showers and prolonged juvenile sulks.
The clouds have no reserve, no dignity; if there is

a drop of water in them (and there generally are several drops), out it comes. The prettiest little showers march across the country in summer, scarcely bigger than a street watering-cart; sometimes by getting over the fence one can avoid them, but they keep the haymakers in a perpetual flurry. There is no cloud scenery, as with us, no mass and solidity, no height nor depth. The clouds seem low, vague, and vapory, — immature, indefinite, inconsequential, like youth.

The walk to Selborne was through mist and light rain. Few bird voices, save the cries of the lapwing and the curlew, were heard. Shortly after leaving Liphook the road takes a straight cut for three or four miles through a level, black, barren, peaty stretch of country, with Wolmer Forest a short distance on the right. Under the low-hanging clouds the scene was a dismal one, — a black earth beneath and a gloomy sky above. For miles the only sign of life was a baker's cart rattling along the smooth, white road. At the end of this solitude I came to cultivated fields, and a little hamlet and an inn. At this inn (for a wonder!) I got some breakfast. The family had not yet had theirs, and I sat with them at the table, and had substantial fare. From this point I followed a footpath a couple of miles through fields and parks. The highways for the most part seemed so narrow and exclusive, or inclusive, such penalties seemed to attach to a view over the high walls and hedges that shut me in, that a footpath was always a wel-

come escape to me. I opened the wicket or
mounted the stile without much concern as to
whether it would further me on my way or not.
It was like turning the flank of an enemy. These
well-kept fields and lawns, these cozy nooks, these
stately and exclusive houses that had taken such
pains to shut out the public gaze, — from the footpath one had them at an advantage, and could
pluck out their mystery. On striking the highway
again, I met the postmistress, stepping briskly
along with the morning mail. Her husband had
died, and she had taken his place as mail-carrier.
England is so densely populated, the country is so
like a great city suburb, that your mail is brought
to your door everywhere, the same as in town. I
walked a distance with a boy driving a little old
white horse with a cart-load of brick. He lived at
Hedleigh, six miles distant; he had left there at
five o'clock in the morning, and had heard a nightingale. He was sure; as I pressed him, he described the place minutely. "She was in the large
fir-tree by Tom Anthony's gate, at the south end
of the village." Then, I said, doubtless I shall
find one in some of Gilbert White's haunts; but I
did not. I spent two rainy days at Selborne; I
passed many chilly and cheerless hours loitering
along those wet lanes and dells and dripping hang-
ers, wooing both my bird and the spirit of the gentle parson, but apparently without getting very
near to either. When I think of the place now, I
see its hurrying and anxious haymakers in the field

of mown grass, and hear the cry of a child that sat in the hay back of the old church, and cried by the hour while its mother was busy with her rake not far off. The rain had ceased, the hay had dried off a little, and scores of men, women, and children, but mostly women, had flocked to the fields to rake it up. The hay is got together inch by inch, and every inch is fought for. They first rake it up into narrow swaths, each person taking a strip about a yard wide. If they hold the ground thus gained, when the hay dries an hour or two longer, they take another hitch, and thus on till they get it into the cock or "carry" it from the windrow. It is usually nearly worn out with handling before they get it into the rick.

From Selborne I went to Alton, along a road that was one prolonged rifle-pit, but smooth and hard as a rock; thence by train back to London. To leave no ground for self-accusation in future, on the score of not having made a thorough effort to hear my songster, I the next day made a trip north toward Cambridge, leaving the train at Hitchin, a large picturesque old town, and thought myself in just the right place at last. I found a road between the station and the town proper called Nightingale Lane, famous for its songsters. A man who kept a thrifty-looking inn on the corner (where, by the way, I was again refused both bed and board) said they sang night and morning in the trees opposite. He had heard them the night before, but had not noticed them that morning. He often sat at night

with his friends, with open windows, listening to
the strain.   He said he had tried several times to
hold his breath as long as the bird did in uttering
certain notes, but could not do it.   This, I knew,
was an exaggeration; but I waited eagerly for nightfall, and, when it came, paced the street like a patrol-
man, and paced other streets, and lingered about
other likely localities, but caught nothing but
neuralgic pains in my shoulder.   I had no better
success in the morning, and here gave over the
pursuit, saying to myself, It matters little, after
all; I have seen the country and had some object
for a walk, and that is sufficient.

Altogether I heard the bird less than five minutes, and only a few bars of its song, but enough
to satisfy me of the surprising quality of the strain.

It had the master tone as clearly as Tennyson
or any great prima donna or famous orator has it.
Indeed, it was just the same.   Here is the complete artist, of whom all these other birds are but
hints and studies.   Bright, startling, assured, of
great compass and power, it easily dominates all
other notes; the harsher *chur-r-r-r-rg* notes serve
as foil to her surpassing brilliancy.   Wordsworth,
among the poets, has hit off the song nearest: —

> "Those notes of thine, — they pierce and pierce;
> Tumultuous harmony and fierce !"

I could easily understand that this bird might
keep people awake at night by singing near their
houses, as I was assured it frequently does; there
is something in the strain so startling and awaken-

ing. Its start is a vivid flash of sound. On the whole, a high-bred, courtly, chivalrous song; a song for ladies to hear leaning from embowered windows on moonlight nights; a song for royal parks and groves, — and easeful but impassioned life. We have no bird-voice so piercing and loud, with such flexibility and compass, such full-throated harmony and long-drawn cadences; though we have songs of more melody, tenderness, and plaintiveness. None but the nightingale could have inspired Keats's ode, — that longing for self-forgetfulness and for the oblivion of the world, to escape the fret and fever of life.

"And with thee fade away into the forest dim."

V

ENGLISH AND AMERICAN SONG—BIRDS

THE charm of the songs of birds, like that of a nation's popular airs and hymns, is so little a question of intrinsic musical excellence, and so largely a matter of association and suggestion, or of subjective coloring and reminiscence, that it is perhaps entirely natural for every people to think their own feathered songsters the best. What music would there not be to the homesick American, in Europe, in the simple and plaintive note of our bluebird, or the ditty of our song sparrow, or the honest carol of our robin; and what, to the European traveler in this country, in the burst of the black-cap, or the redbreast, or the whistle of the merlin! The relative merit of bird-songs can hardly be settled dogmatically; I suspect there is very little of what we call music, or of what could be noted on the musical scale, in even the best of them; they are parts of nature, and their power is in the degree in which they speak to our experience.

When the Duke of Argyll, who is a lover of the birds and a good ornithologist, was in this country, he got the impression that our song-birds were inferior to the British, and he refers to others of his countrymen as of like opinion. No wonder he thought our robin inferior in power to the missel thrush, in variety to the mavis, and in melody to the blackbird! Robin did not and could not sing to his ears the song he sings to ours. Then it is very likely true that his grace did not hear the robin in the most opportune moment and season, or when the contrast of his song with the general silence and desolation of nature is the most striking and impressive. The nightingale needs to be heard at night, the lark at dawn rising to meet the sun; and robin, if you would know the magic of his voice, should be heard in early spring, when, as the sun is setting, he carols steadily for ten or fifteen minutes from the top of some near tree. There is perhaps no other sound in nature; patches of snow linger here and there; the trees are naked and the eartn is cold and dead, and this contented, hopeful, reassuring, and withal musical strain, poured out so freely and deliberately, fills the void with the very breath and presence of the spring. It is a simple strain, well suited to the early season; there are no intricacies in it, but its honest cheer and directness, with its slight plaintive tinge, like that of the sun gilding the treetops, go straight to the heart. The compass and variety of the robin's powers are not to be despised either. A German who has great skill in the musical education of birds told me what I was surprised to hear, namely, that our robin surpasses the European blackbird in capabilities of voice.

The duke does not mention by name all the
birds he heard while in this country. He was evidently influenced in his opinion of them by the fact
that our common sandpiper appeared to be a silent
bird, whereas its British cousin, the sandpiper of
the lakes and streams of the Scottish Highlands, is
very loquacious, and the "male bird has a continuous and most lively song." Either the duke must
have seen our bird in one of its silent and meditative moods, or else, in the wilds of Canada where
his grace speaks of having seen it, the sandpiper is
a more taciturn bird than it is in the States. True,
its call-notes are not incessant, and it is not properly a song-bird any more than the British species
is; but it has a very pretty and pleasing note as it
flits up and down our summer streams, or runs
along on their gray, pebbly, and bowlder-strewn
shallows. I often hear its calling and piping at
night during its spring migratings. Indeed, we
have no silent bird that I am aware of, though our
pretty cedar-bird has, perhaps, the least voice of
any. A lady writes me that she has heard the
hummingbird sing, and says she is not to be put
down, even if I were to prove by the anatomy of
the bird's vocal organs that a song was impossible
to it.

Argyll says that, though he was in the woods and
fields of Canada and of the States in the richest
moment of the spring, he heard little of that burst
of song which in England comes from the blackcap,
and the garden warbler, and the whitethroat, and

the reed warbler, and the common wren, and (locally) from the nightingale. There is no lack of a burst of song in this country (except in the remote forest solitudes) during the richest moment of the spring, say from the 1st to the 20th of May, and at times till near midsummer; moreover, more bird-voices join in it, as I shall point out, than in Britain; but it is probably more fitful and intermittent, more confined to certain hours of the day, and probably proceeds from throats less loud and vivacious than that with which our distinguished critic was familiar. The ear hears best and easiest what it has heard before. Properly to apprehend and appreciate bird-songs, especially to disentangle them from the confused murmur of nature, requires more or less familiarity with them. If the duke had passed a season with us in some *one* place in the country, in New York or New England, he would probably have modified his views about the silence of our birds.

One season, early in May, I discovered an English skylark in full song above a broad, low meadow in the midst of a landscape that possessed features attractive to a great variety of our birds. Every morning for many days I used to go and sit on the brow of a low hill that commanded the field, or else upon a gentle swell in the midst of the meadow itself, and listen to catch the song of the lark. The maze and tangle of bird-voices and bird-choruses through which my ear groped its way searching for the new song can be imagined when I say

that within hearing there were from fifteen to
twenty different kinds of songsters, all more or less
in full tune.   If their notes and calls could have
been materialized and made as palpable to the eye
as they were to the ear, I think they would have
veiled the landscape and darkened the day.   There
were big songs and little songs, — songs from the
trees, the bushes, the ground, the air, — warbles,
trills, chants, musical calls, and squeals, etc.   Near
by in the foreground were the catbird and the brown
thrasher, the former in the bushes, the latter on the
top of a hickory.   These birds are related to the
mockingbird, and may be called performers; their
songs are a series of vocal feats, like the exhibition
of an acrobat; they throw musical somersaults, and
turn and twist and contort themselves in a very edi-
fying manner, with now and then a ventriloquial
touch.   The catbird is the more shrill, supple, and
feminine; the thrasher the louder, richer, and more
audacious.   The mate of the latter had a nest,
which I found in a field under the spreading ground-
juniper.   From several points along the course of
a bushy little creek there came a song, or a melody
of notes and calls, that also put me out, — the tipsy,
hodge-podge strain of the polyglot chat, a strong,
olive-backed, yellow - breasted, black - billed bird,
with a voice like that of a jay or a crow that had
been to school to a robin or an oriole, — a performer
sure to arrest your ear and sure to elude your eye.
There is no bird so afraid of being seen, or fonder
of being heard.

The golden voice of the wood thrush that came
to me from the border of the woods on my right
was no hindrance to the ear, it was so serene,
liquid, and, as it were, transparent: the lark's song
has nothing in common with it. Neither were the
songs of the many bobolinks in the meadow at all
confusing, — a brief tinkle of silver bells in the
grass, while I was listening for a sound more like
the sharp and continuous hum of silver wheels upon
a pebbly beach. Certain notes of the red-shouldered starlings in the alders and swamp maples near
by, the distant barbaric voice of the great crested
flycatcher, the jingle of the kingbird, the shrill,
metallic song of the savanna sparrow, and the piercing call of the meadowlark, all stood more or less
in the way of the strain I was listening for, because
every one had a touch of that burr or guttural hum
of the lark's song. The ear had still other notes
to contend with, as the strong, bright warble of the
tanager, the richer and more melodious strain of
the rose-breasted grosbeak, the distant, brief, and
emphatic song of the chewink, the child-like contented warble of the red-eyed vireo, the animated
strain of the goldfinch, the softly ringing notes of
the bush sparrow, the rapid, circling, vivacious
strain of the purple finch, the gentle lullaby of the
song sparrow, the pleasing "wichery," "wichery"
of the yellow-throat, the clear whistle of the oriole,
the loud call of the high-hole, the squeak and chat-
ter of swallows, etc. But when the lark did rise
in full song, it was easy to hear him athwart all

these various sounds, first, because of the sense of altitude his strain had, — its skyward character, — and then because of its loud, aspirated, penetrating, unceasing, jubilant quality. It cut its way to the ear like something exceeding swift, sharp, and copious. It overtook and outran every other sound; it had an undertone like the humming of multitudinous wheels and spindles. Now and then some turn would start and set off a new combination of shriller or of graver notes, but all of the same precipitate, out-rushing and down-pouring character; not, on the whole, a sweet or melodious song, but a strong and blithe one.

The duke is abundantly justified in saying that we have no bird in this country, at least east of the Mississippi, that can fill the place of the skylark. Our high, wide, bright skies seem his proper field, too. His song is a pure ecstasy, untouched by any plaintiveness, or pride, or mere hilarity, — a wellspring of morning joy and blitheness set high above the fields and downs. Its effect is well suggested in this stanza of Wordsworth: —

> "Up with me! up with me into the clouds!
>   For thy song, Lark, is strong;
> Up with me, up with me into the clouds!
>   Singing, singing,
> With clouds and sky about thee ringing,
>   Lift me, guide me till I find
> That spot which seems so to thy mind!"

But judging from Gilbert White's and Barrington's lists, I should say that our bird-choir was a larger one, and embraced more good songsters, than the British.

White names twenty-two species of birds that sing in England during the spring and summer, including the swallow in the list. A list of the spring and summer songsters in New York and New England, without naming any that are characteristically wood-birds, like the hermit thrush and veery, the two wagtails, the thirty or more warblers, and the solitary vireo, or including any of the birds that have musical call-notes, and by some are denominated songsters, as the bluebird, the sandpiper, the swallow, the red-shouldered starling, the pewee, the high-hole, and others, would embrace more names, though perhaps no songsters equal to the lark and nightingale, to wit: the robin, the catbird, the Baltimore oriole, the orchard oriole, the song sparrow, the wood sparrow, the vesper sparrow, the social sparrow, the swamp sparrow, the purple finch, the wood thrush, the scarlet tanager, the indigo-bird, the goldfinch, the bobolink, the summer yellowbird, the meadowlark, the house wren, the marsh wren, the brown thrasher, the chewink, the chat, the red-eyed vireo, the white-eyed vireo, the Maryland yellow-throat, and the rose-breasted grosbeak.

The British sparrows are for the most part songless. What a ditty is that of our song sparrow, rising from the garden fence or the roadside so early in March, so prophetic and touching, with endless variations and pretty trilling effects; or the song of the vesper sparrow, full of the repose and the wild sweetness of the fields; or the strain of the little bush sparrow, suddenly projected upon the silence of the fields or of the evening twilight, and delighting the ear as a beautiful scroll delights the eye! The white-crowned, the white-throated, and the Canada sparrows sing transiently spring and fall; and I have heard the fox sparrow in April, when his song haunted my heart like some bright, sad, delicious memory of youth, — the richest and most moving of all sparrow-songs.

Our wren-music, too, is superior to anything of the kind in the Old World, because we have a greater variety of wren-songsters. Our house wren is inferior to the British house wren, but our marsh wren has a lively song; while our winter wren, in sprightliness, mellowness, plaintiveness, and execution, is surpassed by but few songsters in the world. The summer haunts of this wren are our high, cool, northern woods, where, for the most part, his music is lost on the primeval solitude.

The British flycatcher, according to White, is a silent bird, while our species, as the phœbe-bird, the wood pewee, the kingbird, the little green flycatcher, and others, all have notes more or less lively and musical. The great crested flycatcher has a harsh voice, but the pathetic and silvery note of the wood pewee more than makes up for it. White says the golden-crowned wren is not a song-bird in Great Britain. The corresponding species here has a pleasing though not remarkable song, which is seldom heard, however, except in its breeding haunts in the north. But its congener, the ruby-

crowned kinglet, has a rich, delicious, and prolonged
warble, which is noticeable in the Northern States
for a week or two in April or May, while the bird
pauses to feed on its way to its summer home.

There are no vireos in Europe, nor birds that
answer to them. With us, they contribute an important element to the music of our groves and
woods. There are few birds I should miss more
than the red-eyed vireo, with his cheerful musical
soliloquy, all day and all summer, in the maples
and locusts. It is he, or rather she, that builds
the exquisite basket nest on the ends of the low,
leafy branches, suspending it between two twigs.
The warbling vireo has a stronger, louder strain,
more continuous, but not quite so sweet. The solitary vireo is heard only in the deep woods, while
the white-eyed is still more local or restricted in
its range, being found only in wet, bushy places,
whence its vehement, varied, and brilliant song is
sure to catch the dullest ear.

The goldfinches of the two countries, though
differing in plumage, are perhaps pretty evenly
matched in song; while our purple finch, or linnet,
I am persuaded, ranks far above the English linnet, or lintie, as the Scotch call it. In compass, in
melody, in sprightliness, it is a remarkable songster.
Indeed, take the finches as a family, they certainly
furnish more good songsters in this country than in
Great Britain. They furnish the staple of our bird-
melody, including in the family the tanager and
the grosbeaks, while in Europe the warblers lead.

White names seven finches in his list, and Barrington includes eight, none of them very noted songsters, except the linnet. Our list would include the sparrows above named, and the indigo-bird, the goldfinch, the purple finch, the scarlet tanager, the rose-breasted grosbeak, the blue grosbeak, and the cardinal bird. Of these birds, all except the fox sparrow and the blue grosbeak are familiar summer songsters throughout the Middle and Eastern States. The indigo-bird is a midsummer and an all-summer songster of great brilliancy. So is the tanager. I judge there is no European thrush that, in the pure charm of melody and hymn-like serenity and spirituality, equals our wood and hermit thrushes, as there is no bird there that, in simple lingual excellence, approaches our bobolink.

The European cuckoo makes more music than ours, and their robin redbreast is a better singer than the allied species, to wit, the bluebird, with us. But it is mainly in the larks and warblers that the European birds are richer in songsters than are ours. We have an army of small wood-warblers, — no less than forty species, — but most of them have faint chattering or lisping songs that escape all but the most attentive ear, and then they spend the summer far to the north. Our two wagtails are our most brilliant warblers, if we except the kinglets, which are Northern birds in summer, and the Kentucky warbler, which is a Southern bird; but they probably do not match the English blackcap, or whitethroat, or garden warbler, to say nothing of the nightingale, though Audubon thought our large-billed water-thrush, or wagtail, equaled that famous bird. It is certainly a brilliant songster, but most provokingly brief; the ear is arrested by a sudden joyous burst of melody proceeding from the dim aisles along which some wild brook has its way, but just as you say "Listen!" it ceases. I hear and see the bird every season along a rocky stream that flows through a deep chasm amid a wood of hemlock and pine. As I sit at the foot of some cascade, or on the brink of some little dark eddying pool above it, this bird darts by me, up or down the stream, or alights near me, upon a rock or stone at the edge of the water. Its speckled breast, its dark olive-colored back, its teetering, mincing gait, like that of a sandpiper, and its sharp *chit*, like the click of two pebbles under water, are characteristic features. Then its quick, ringing song, which you are sure presently to hear, suggests something so bright and silvery that it seems almost to light up, for a brief moment, the dim retreat. If this strain were only sustained and prolonged like the nightingale's, there would be good grounds for Audubon's comparison. Its cousin, the wood wagtail, or golden-crowned thrush of the older ornithologists, and golden-crowned accentor of the later, — a common bird in all our woods, — has a similar strain, which it delivers as it were surreptitiously, and in the most precipitate manner, while on the wing, high above the treetops. It is a kind of wood-lark, practicing and rehearsing on the sly. When the modest

songster is ready to come out and give all a chance
to hear his full and completed strain, the European
wood-lark will need to look to his laurels.   These
two birds are our best warblers, and yet they are
probably seldom heard, except by persons who know
and admire them.   If the two kinglets could also
be included in our common New England summer
residents, our warbler music would only pale before
the song of Philomela herself.   The English red-
start evidently surpasses ours as a songster, and we
have no bird to match the English wood-lark above
referred to, which is said to be but little inferior
to the skylark; but, on the other hand, besides the
sparrows and vireos, already mentioned, they have
no songsters to match our oriole, our orchard starling, our catbird, our brown thrasher (second only
to the mockingbird), our chewink, our snowbird, our
cow-bunting, our bobolink, and our yellow-breasted
chat.   As regards the swallows of the two countries,
the advantage is rather on the side of the American.
Our chimney swallow, with his incessant, silvery,
rattling chipper, evidently makes more music than
the corresponding house swallow of Europe; while our
purple martin is not represented in the Old World
avifauna at all.   And yet it is probably true that a
dweller in England hears more bird-music throughout the year than a dweller in this country, and that
which, in some respects, is of a superior order.

In the first place, there is not so much of it lost
"upon the desert air," upon the wild, unlistening
solitudes.   The English birds are more domestic

and familiar than ours; more directly and intimately
associated with man; not, as a class, so withdrawn
and lost in the great void of the wild and the unreclaimed.   England is like a continent concentrated,
— all the waste land, the barren stretches, the wildernesses, left out.   The birds are brought near
together and near to man.   Wood-birds here are
house and garden birds there.   They find good
pasturage and protection everywhere.   A land of
parks, and gardens, and hedge-rows, and game pre-
serves, and a climate free from violent extremes, —
what a stage for the birds, and for enhancing the
effect of their songs!   How prolific they are, how
abundant!   If our songsters were hunted and
trapped by bird-fanciers and others, as the lark,
and goldfinch, and mavis, etc., are in England, the
race would soon become extinct.   Then, as a rule,
it is probably true that the British birds as a class
have more voice than ours have, or certain qualities
that make their songs more striking and conspicuous, such as greater vivacity and strength.   They
are less bright in plumage, but more animated in
voice.   They are not so recently out of the woods,
and their strains have not that elusiveness and
plaintiveness that ours have.   They sing with more
confidence and copiousness, and as if they, too, had
been touched by civilization.

Then they sing more hours in the day, and more
days in the year.   This is owing to the milder and
more equable climate.   I heard the skylark singing
above the South Downs in October, apparently with

full spring fervor and delight. The wren, the
robin, and the wood-lark sing throughout the winter, and in midsummer there are perhaps more
vocal throats than here. The heat and blaze of our
midsummer sun silence most of our birds.

There are but four songsters that I hear with any
regularity after the meridian of summer is past,
namely, the indigo-bird, the wood or bush sparrow,
the scarlet tanager, and the red-eyed vireo, while
White names eight or nine August songsters, though
he speak of the yellow-hammer only as persistent.
His dictum, that birds sing as long as nidification
goes on, is as true here as in England. Hence our
wood thrush will continue in song over into August
if, as frequently happens, its June nest has been
broken up by the crows or squirrels.

The British songsters are more vocal at night
than ours. White says the grasshopper lark chirps
all night in the height of summer. The sedge-bird
also sings the greater part of the night. A stone
thrown into the bushes where it is roosting, after
it has become silent, will set it going again. Other
British birds, besides the nightingale, sing more or
less at night.

In this country the mockingbird is the only regular night-singer we have. Other songsters break
out occasionally in the middle of the night, but so
briefly that it gives one the impression that they
sing in their sleep. Thus I have heard the hair-
bird, or chippie, the kingbird, the oven-bird, and
the cuckoo fitfully in the dead of the night, like a
schoolboy laughing in his dreams.

On the other hand, there are certain aspects in which our songsters appear to advantage. That they surpass the European species in sweetness, tenderness, and melody I have no doubt; and that our mockingbird, in his native haunts in the South, surpasses any bird in the world in fluency, variety, and execution is highly probable. That the total effect of his strain may be less winning and persuasive than the nocturne of the nightingale is the only question in my mind about the relative merits of the two songsters. Bring our birds together as they are brought together in England, let all our shy wood-birds — like the hermit thrush, the veery, the winter wren, the wood wagtail, the water wagtail, the many warblers, the several vireos — become birds of the groves and orchards, and there would be a burst of song indeed.

Bates, the naturalist of the Amazon, speaks of a little thrush he used to hear in his rambles that showed the American quality to which I have referred. "It is a much smaller and plainer-colored bird," he says, "than our [the English] thrush, and its song is not so loud, varied, or so long sustained; here the tone is of a sweet and plaintive quality, which harmonizes well with the wild and silent woodlands, where alone it is heard in the mornings and evenings of sultry, tropical days."

I append parallel lists of the better-known American and English song-birds, marking in each with an asterisk, those that are probably the better songsters; followed by a list of other American songsters, some of which are not represented in the British avifauna: —

Old England.	New England.
* Wood-lark.	Meadowlark.
Song-thrush.	* Wood thrush.
* Jenny Wren.	House wren.
Willow wren.	* Winter wren.
* Redbreast.	Bluebird.
* Redstart.	Redstart.
Hedge-sparrow.	* Song sparrow.
Yellow-hammer.	* Fox sparrow.
* Skylark.	Bobolink.
Swallow.	Swallow.
* Blackcap.	Wood wagtail.
Titlark.	Titlark (spring and fall).
* Blackbird.	Robin.
Whitethroat.	* Maryland yellow-throat.
Goldfinch.	Goldfinch.
Greenfinch.	* Wood sparrow.
Reed-sparrow.	* Vesper sparrow.
Linnet.	* Purple finch.
* Chaffinch.	Indigo-bird.
* Nightingale.	Water wagtail.
Missel thrush.	* Hermit thrush.
Great titmouse.	Savanna sparrow.
Bullfinch.	Chickadee.

New England song-birds not included in the above are: —

Red-eyed vireo.	Orchard oriole.
White-eyed vireo.	Catbird.
Brotherly love vireo.	Brown thrasher.
Solitary vireo.	Chewink.
Yellow-throated vireo.	Rose-breasted grosbeak.
Scarlet tanager.	Purple martin.
Baltimore oriole.	Mockingbird (occasionally).

Besides these, a dozen or more species of the Mniotiltidæ, or wood-warblers, might be named, some of which, like the black-throated green warbler, the speckled Canada warbler, the hooded warbler, the mourning ground-warbler, and the yellow warbler, are fine songsters.

VI

IMPRESSIONS OF SOME ENGLISH BIRDS

THE foregoing chapter was written previous to my last visit to England, and when my knowledge of the British song-birds was mainly from report, and not from personal observation. I had heard the skylark, and briefly the robin, and snatches of a few other bird strains, while in that country in the autumn of 1871; but of the full spring and summer chorus, and the merits of the individual songsters, I knew little except through such writers as White, Broderip, and Barrington. Hence, when I found myself upon British soil once more, and the birds in the height of their May jubilee, I improved my opportunities, and had very soon traced every note home. It is not a long and difficult lesson; there is not a great variety of birds, and they do not hide in woods and remote corners. You find them nearly all wherever your walk leads you. And how they do sing! how loud and piercing their notes are! Not a little of the pleasure I felt arose from the fact that the birds sang much as I expected them to, much as they ought to have sung according to my previous views of their merits and qualities, when contrasted with our own songsters.

I shall not soon forget how my ears were beset that bright May morning, two days after my arrival at Glasgow, when I walked from Ayr to Alloway, a course of three miles in one of the most charming and fertile rural districts in Scotland. It was as warm as mid-June, and the country had the most leafy and luxuriant June aspect. Above a broad stretch of undulating meadow-land on my right the larks were in full song. These I knew; these I welcomed. What a sound up there, as if the sunshine were vocal! A little farther along, in a clover field, I heard my first corn-crake. "Crex, crex, crex," came the harsh note out of the grass, like the rasping sound of some large insect, and I knew the bird at once. But when I came to a beautiful grove or wood, jealously guarded by a wall twelve feet high (some fine house concealed back there, I saw by the entrance), what a throng of strange songs and calls beset my ears! The concert was at its height. The wood fairly rang and reverberated with bird-voices. How loud, how vivacious, almost clamorous, they sounded to me! I paused in delightful bewilderment.

Two or three species of birds, as I afterwards found, were probably making all the music I heard, and of these, one species was contributing at least two thirds of it. At Alloway I tarried nearly a week, putting up at a neat little inn

     "Where Doon rins, wimplin', clear,"

and I was not long in analyzing this spirited bird-choir, and tracing each note home to its proper

source. It was, indeed, a burst of song, as the
Duke of Argyll had said, but the principal singer
his grace does not mention. Indeed, nothing I
had read, or could find in the few popular treatises
on British ornithology I carried about with me,
had given me any inkling of which was the most
abundant and vociferous English song-bird, any
more than what I had read or heard had given me
any idea of which was the most striking and conspicuous wild flower, or which the most universal
weed. Now the most abundant song-bird in Britain
is the chaffinch, the most conspicuous wild flower
(at least in those parts of the country I saw) is the
foxglove, and the most ubiquitous weed is the
nettle. Throughout the month of May, and probably during all the spring months, the chaffinch
makes two thirds of the music that ordinarily greets
the ear as one walks or drives about the country.
In both England and Scotland, in my walks up to
the time of my departure, the last of July, I seemed
to see three chaffinches to one of any other species
of bird. It is a permanent resident in this island,
and in winter appears in immense flocks. The
male is the prettiest of British song-birds, with its
soft blue-gray back, barred wings, and pink breast
and sides. The Scotch call it shilfa. At Alloway
there was a shilfa for every tree, and its hurried and
incessant notes met and intersected each other from
all directions every moment of the day, like wave-
lets on a summer pool. So many birds, and each
one so persistent and vociferous, accounts for their

part in the choir.   The song is as loud as that of
our orchard starling, and is even more animated.
It begins with a rapid, wren-like trill, which
quickly becomes a sharp jingle, then slides into a
warble, and ends with an abrupt flourish.   I have
never heard a song that began so liltingly end with
such a quick, abrupt emphasis.   The last note often
sounds like "whittier," uttered with great sharp-
ness; but one that used to sing in an apple-tree
over my head, day after day there by the Doon,
finished its strain each time with the sharp ejacula-
tion, "Sister, right here."   Afterwards, whenever
I met a shilfa, I could hear in its concluding note
this pointed and almost impatient exclamation of
"Sister, right here."   The song, on the whole, is
a pleasing one, and very characteristic; so rapid,
incessant, and loud.   The bird seemed to be held
in much less esteem in Britain than on the Continent, where it is much sought after as a caged bird.
In Germany, in the forest of Thuringia, the bird is
in such quest that scarcely can one be heard.   A
common workman has been known to give his cow
for a favorite songster.   The chaffinch has far less
melody and charm of song than some of our finches,
notably our purple finch; but it is so abundant and
so persistent in song that in quantity of music it
far excels any singer we have.

Next to the chaffinch in the volume of its song,
and perhaps in some localities surpassing it, is the
song-thrush.   I did not find this bird upon the
Doon, and but rarely in other places in Scotland,

but in the south of England it leads the choir. Its voice can be heard above all others. But one would never suspect it to be a thrush. It has none of the flute-like melody and serene, devotional quality of our thrush strains. It is a shrill whistling polyglot. Its song is much after the manner of that of our brown thrasher, made up of vocal attitudes and poses. It is easy to translate its strain into various words or short ejaculatory sentences. It sings till the darkness begins to deepen, and I could fancy what the young couple walking in the gloaming would hear from the trees overhead. "Kiss her, kiss her; do it, do it; be quick, be quick; stick her to it, stick her to it; that was neat, that was neat; that will do," with many other calls not so explicit, and that might sometimes be construed as approving nods or winks. Sometimes it has a staccato whistle. Its performance is always animated, loud, and clear, but never, to my ear, melodious, as the poets so often have it. Even Burns says, —

"The mavis mild and mellow."

Drayton hits it when he says, —

"The throstle with shrill sharps," etc.

Ben Jonson's "lusty throstle" is still better. It is a song of great strength and unbounded good cheer; it proceeds from a sound heart and a merry throat. There is no touch of plaintiveness or melancholy in it; it is as expressive of health and good digestion as the crowing of the cock in the morning. When I was hunting for the nightingale, the thrush frequently made such a din just at dusk as to be a great annoyance. At Kew, where I passed a few weeks, its shrill pipe usually woke me in the morning.

A thrush of a much mellower strain is the black-bird, which is our robin cut in ebony. His golden bill gives a golden touch to his song. It was the most leisurely strain I heard. Amid the loud, vivacious, workaday chorus, it had an easeful, *dolce far niente* effect. I place the song before that of our robin, where it belongs in quality, but it falls short in some other respects. It constantly seemed to me as if the bird was a learner and had not yet mastered his art. The tone is fine, but the execution is labored; the musician does not handle his instrument with deftness and confidence. It seems as if the bird were trying to whistle some simple air, and never quite succeeding. Parts of the song are languid and feeble, and the whole strain is wanting in the decision and easy fulfillment of our robin's song. The bird is noisy and tuneful in the twilight like his American congener.

Such British writers on birds and bird life as I have been able to consult do not, it seems to me, properly discriminate and appreciate the qualities and merits of their own songsters. The most melodious strain I heard, and the only one that exhibited to the full the best qualities of the American songsters, proceeded from a bird quite unknown to fame, in the British Islands at least. I refer to the willow warbler. or willow wren as it is also called, — a little brown bird, that builds a dome-shaped nest upon the ground and lines it with feathers. White says it has a "sweet, plaintive note," which is but half the truth. It has a long, tender, delicious warble, not wanting in strength and volume, but eminently pure and sweet, — the song of the chaffinch refined and idealized. The famous blackcap, which I heard in the south of England and again in France, falls far short of it in these respects, and only surpasses it in strength and brilliancy. The song is, perhaps, in the minor key, feminine and not masculine, but it touches the heart.

"That strain again; it had a dying fall."

The song of the willow warbler has a dying fall; no other bird-song is so touching in this respect. It mounts up round and full, then runs down the scale, and expires upon the air in a gentle murmur. I heard the bird everywhere; next to the chaffinch, its voice greeted my ear oftenest; yet many country people of whom I inquired did not know the bird, or confounded it with some other. It is too fine a song for the ordinary English ear; there is not noise enough in it. The whitethroat is much more famous; it has a louder, coarser voice; it sings with great emphasis and assurance, and is a much better John Bull than the little willow warbler.

I could well understand, after being in England a few days, why, to English travelers, our songsters seem inferior to their own. They are much less loud and vociferous. less abundant and familiar:

one needs to woo them more; they are less recently out of the wilderness; their songs have the delicacy and wildness of most woodsy forms, and are as plaintive as the whistle of the wind. They are not so happy a race as the English songsters, as if life had more trials for them, as doubtless it has in their enforced migrations and in the severer climate with which they have to contend.

When one hears the European cuckoo he regrets that he has ever heard a cuckoo clock. The clock has stolen the bird's thunder; and when you hear the rightful owner, the note has a second-hand, artificial sound. It is only another cuckoo clock off there on the hill or in the grove. Yet it is a cheerful call, with none of the solitary and monkish character of our cuckoo's note; and, as it comes early in spring, I can see how much it must mean to native ears.

I found that the only British song-bird I had done injustice to in my previous estimate was the wren. It is far superior to our house wren. It approaches very nearly our winter wren, if it does not equal it. Without hearing the two birds together, it would be impossible to decide which was the better songster. Its strain has the same gushing, lyrical character, and the shape, color, and manner of the two birds are nearly identical. It is very common, sings everywhere, and therefore contributes much more to the general entertainment than does our bird. Barrington marks the wren far too low in his table of the comparative merit of British song-birds; he denies it mellowness and plaintiveness, and makes it high only in sprightliness, a fact that discredits his whole table. He makes the thrush and blackbird equal in the two qualities first named, which is equally wide of the mark.

The English robin is a better songster than I expected to find him. The poets and writers have not done him justice. . He is of the royal line of the nightingale, and inherits some of the qualities of that famous bird. His favorite hour for singing is the gloaming, and I used to hear him the last of all. His song is peculiar, jerky, and spasmodic, but abounds in the purest and most piercing tones to be heard, — piercing from their smoothness, intensity, and fullness of articulation; rapid and crowded at one moment, as if some barrier had suddenly given way, then as suddenly pausing, and scintillating at intervals, bright, tapering shafts of sound. It stops and hesitates, and blurts out its notes like a stammerer; but when they do come they are marvelously clear and pure. I have heard green hickory branches thrown into a fierce blaze jet out the same fine, intense, musical sounds on the escape of the imprisoned vapors in the hard wood as characterize the robin's song.

One misses along English fields and highways the tender music furnished at home by our sparrows, and in the woods and groves the plaintive cries of our pewees and the cheerful soliloquy of our red-eyed vireo. The English sparrows and buntings are harsh-voiced, and their songs, when they have songs, are crude. The yellow-hammer comes nearest to our typical sparrow, it is very common, and is a persistent songster, but the song is slight, like that of our savanna sparrow — scarcely more than the chirping of a grasshopper. In form and color it is much like our vesper sparrow, except that the head of the male has a light yellow tinge.

The greenfinch or green linnet is an abundant bird everywhere, but its song is less pleasing than that of several of our finches. The goldfinch is very rare, mainly, perhaps, because it is so persistently trapped by bird-fanciers; its song is a series of twitters and chirps, less musical to my ear than that of our goldfinch, especially when a flock of the latter are congregated in a tree and inflating their throats in rivalry. Their golden-crowned kinglet has a fine thread-like song, far less than that of our kinglet, less even than that of our black and white creeper. The nuthatch has not the soft, clear call of ours, and the various woodpeckers figure much less; there is less wood to peck, and they seem a more shy and silent race. I saw but one in all my walks, and that was near Wolmer Forest. I looked in vain for the wood-lark; the country people confound it with the pipit. The blackcap warbler I found to be a rare and much overpraised bird. The nightingale is very restricted in its range, and is nearly silent by the middle of June. I made a desperate attempt to find it in full song after the seventeenth of the month, as I have

described in a previous chapter, but failed.   And
the garden warbler is by no means found in every
garden; probably I did not hear it more than twice.

The common sandpiper, I should say, was more
loquacious and musical than ours.   I heard it on
the Highland lakes, when its happy notes did indeed
almost run into a song, so continuous and bright
and joyful were they.

One of the first birds I saw, and one of the most
puzzling, was the lapwing or pewit.   I observed it
from the car window, on my way down to Ayr, a
large, broad-winged, awkward sort of bird, like a
cross between a hawk and an owl, swooping and
gamboling in the air as the train darted past.   It
is very abundant in Scotland, especially on the
moors and near the coast.   In the Highlands I saw
them from the top of the stage-coach, running about
the fields with their young.   The most graceful
and pleasing of birds upon the ground, about the
size of the pigeon, now running nimbly along, now
pausing to regard you intently, crested, ringed,
white-bellied, glossy green-backed, with every movement like visible music.   But the moment it
launches into the air its beauty is gone; the wings
look round and clumsy, like a mittened hand, the
tail very short, the head and neck drawn back, with
nothing in the form or movement that suggests the
plover kind.   It gambols and disports itself like
a great bat, which its outlines suggest.   On the
moors I also saw the curlew, and shall never forget
its wild, musical call.

Nearly all the British bird-voices have more of
a burr in them than ours have. Can it be that,
like the people, they speak more from the throat?
It is especially noticeable in the crow tribe, — in
the rook, the jay, the jackdaw. The rook has a
hoarse, thick caw, — not so clearly and roundly
uttered as that of our crow. The swift has a
wheezy, catarrhal squeak, in marked contrast to the
cheery chipper of our swift. In Europe the chimney swallow builds in barns, and the barn swallow
builds in chimneys. The barn swallow, as we
would call it, — chimney swallow, as it is called
there, — is much the same in voice, color, form,
flight, etc., as our bird, while the swift is much
larger than our chimney swallow and has a forked
tail. The martlet, answering to our cliff swallow,
is not so strong and ruddy looking a bird as our
species, but it builds much the same, and has a
similar note. It is more plentiful than our swallow. I was soon struck with the fact that in the
main the British song-birds lead up to and culminate
in two species, namely, in the lark and the nightingale. In these two birds all that is characteristic
in the other songsters is gathered up and carried to
perfection. They crown the series. Nearly all the
finches and pipits seem like rude studies and sketches
of the skylark, and nearly all the warblers and
thrushes point to the nightingale; their powers
have fully blossomed in her. There is nothing in
the lark's song, in the quality or in the manner of
it, that is not sketched or suggested in some voice

lower in the choir, and the tone and compass of the warblers mount in regular gradation from the clinking note of the chiffchaff up to the nightingale. Several of the warblers sing at night, and several of the constituents of the lark sing on the wing. On the lark's side, the birds are remarkable for gladness and ecstacy, and are more creatures of the light and of the open spaces; on the side of the nightingale there is more pure melody, and more a love for the twilight and the privacy of arboreal life. Both the famous songsters are representative as to color, exhibiting the prevailing gray and dark tints. A large number of birds, I noticed, had the two white quills in the tail characteristic of the lark.

I found that I had overestimated the bird-music to be heard in England in midsummer. It appeared to be much less than our own. The last two or three weeks of July were very silent: the only bird I was sure of hearing in my walks was the yellowhammer; while, on returning home early in August, the birds made such music about my house that they woke me up in the morning. The song sparrow and bush sparrow were noticeable till in September, and the red-eyed vireo and warbling vireo were heard daily till in October.

On the whole, I may add that I did not anywhere in England hear so fine a burst of bird-song as I have heard at home, and I listened long for it and attentively. Not so fine in quality, though perhaps greater in quantity. It sometimes happens that several species of our best songsters pass the season in the same locality, some favorite spot in the woods, or at the head of a sheltered valley, that possesses attraction for many kinds. I found such a place one summer by a small mountain lake, in the southern Catskills, just over the farm borders, in the edge of the primitive forest. The lake was surrounded by an amphitheatre of wooded steeps, except a short space on one side where there was an old abandoned clearing, grown up to saplings and brush. Birds love to be near water, and I think they like a good auditorium, love an open space like that of a small lake in the woods, where their voices can have room and their songs reverberate. Certain it is they liked this place, and early in the morning especially, say from half past three to half past four, there was such a burst of melody as I had never before heard. The most prominent voices were those of the wood thrush, veery thrush, rose-breasted grosbeak, winter wren, and one of the vireos, and occasionally at evening that of the hermit, though far off in the dusky background, — birds all notable for their pure melody, except that of the vireo, which was cheery, rather than melodious. A singular song that of this particular vireo, — *" Cheery, cheery, cheery drunk !   Cheery drunk ! "* — all day long in the trees above our tent. The wood thrush was the most abundant, and the purity and eloquence of its strain, or of their mingled strains, heard in the cool dewy morning from across that translucent sheet of water, was indeed memorable. Its liquid and serene melody was in such perfect keeping with the scene.   The eye and the ear both reported the same beauty and harmony. Then the clear, rich fife of the grosbeak from the tops of the tallest trees, the simple flute-like note of the veery, and the sweetly ringing, wildly lyrical outburst of the winter wren, sometimes from the roof of our butternut-colored tent — all joining with it — formed one of the most noteworthy bits of a bird symphony it has ever been my good luck to hear. Often at sundown, too, while we sat idly in our boat, watching the trout break the glassy surface here and there, the same soothing melody would be poured out all around us, and kept up till darkness filled the woods.   The last note would be that of the wood thrush, calling out *"quit,"* *"quit."* Across there in a particular point, I used at night to hear another thrush, the olive-backed, the song a slight variation of the veery's.   I did hear in England in the twilight the robin, blackbird, and song-thrush unite their voices, producing a loud, pleasing chorus; add the nightingale and you have great volume and power, but still the pure melody of my songsters by the lake is probably not reached.

VII

IN WORDSWORTH'S COUNTRY

NO other English poet had touched me quite so closely as Wordsworth. All cultivated men delight in Shakespeare; he is the universal genius; but Wordsworth's poetry has more the character of a message, and a message special and personal, to a comparatively small circle of readers. He stands for a particular phase of human thought and experience, and his service to certain minds is like an initiation into a new order of truths. Note what a revelation he was to the logical mind of John Stuart Mill. His limitations make him all the more private and precious, like the seclusion of one of his mountain dales. He is not and can never be the world's poet, but more especially the poet of those who love solitude and solitary communion with nature. Shakespeare's attitude toward nature is for the most part like that of a gay, careless reveler, who leaves his companions for a moment to pluck a flower or gather a shell here and there, as they stroll

> "By paved fountain, or by rushy brook,
> Or on the beachéd margent of the sea."

He is, of course, preëminent in all purely poetic

achievements, but his poems can never minister to the spirit in the way Wordsworth's do.

One can hardly appreciate the extent to which the latter poet has absorbed and reproduced the spirit of the Westmoreland scenery until he has visited that region. I paused there a few days in early June, on my way south, and again on my return late in July. I walked up from Windermere to Grasmere, where, on the second visit, I took up my abode at the historic Swan Inn, where Scott used to go surreptitiously to get his mug of beer when he was stopping with Wordsworth.

The call of the cuckoo came to me from over Rydal Water as I passed along. I plucked my first foxglove by the roadside; paused and listened to the voice of the mountain torrent; heard

"The cataracts blow their trumpets from the steep;"

caught many a glimpse of green, unpeopled hills, urn-shaped dells, treeless heights, rocky promontories, secluded valleys, and clear, swift-running streams. The scenery was sombre; there were but two colors, green and brown, verging on black; wherever the rock cropped out of the green turf on the mountain-sides, or in the vale, it showed a dark face. But the tenderness and freshness of the green tints were something to remember, — the hue of the first springing April grass, massed and widespread in midsummer.

Then there was a quiet splendor, almost grandeur, about Grasmere vale, such as I had not seen elsewhere, — a kind of monumental beauty and dig-

nity that agreed well with one's conception of the
loftier strains of its poet. It is not too much dominated by the mountains, though shut in on all sides
by them; that stately level floor of the valley keeps
them back and defines them, and they rise from its
outer margin like rugged, green-tufted, and green-
draped walls.

It is doubtless this feature, as De Quincey says,
this floor-like character of the valley, that makes
the scenery of Grasmere more impressive than the
scenery in North Wales, where the physiognomy of
the mountains is essentially the same, but where
the valleys are more bowl-shaped. Amid so much
that is steep and rugged and broken, the eye delights in the repose and equilibrium of horizontal
lines, — a bit of table-land, the surface of the lake,
or the level of the valley bottom. The principal
valleys of our own Catskill region all have this
stately floor, so characteristic of Wordsworth's
country. It was a pleasure which I daily indulged
in to stand on the bridge by Grasmere Church, with
that full, limpid stream before me, pausing and
deepening under the stone embankment near where
the dust of the poet lies, and let the eye sweep
across the plain to the foot of the near mountains,
or dwell upon their encircling summits above the
tops of the trees and the roofs of the village. The
water-ouzel loved to linger there, too, and would sit
in contemplative mood on the stones around which
the water loitered and murmured, its clear white
breast alone defining it from the object upon which

it rested.   Then it would trip along the margin of
the pool, or flit a few feet over its surface, and
suddenly, as if it had burst like a bubble, vanish
before my eyes; there would be a little splash of
the water beneath where I saw it, as if the drop of
which it was composed had reunited with the surface there.   Then, in a moment or two, it would
emerge from the water and take up its stand as dry
and unruffled as ever.   It was always amusing
to see this plump little bird, so unlike a water-fowl
in shape and manner, disappear in the stream.   It
did not seem to dive, but simply dropped into the
water, as if its wings had suddenly failed it.   Sometimes it fairly tumbled in from its perch.   It was
gone from sight in a twinkling, and, while you
were wondering how it could accomplish the feat of
walking on the bottom of the stream under there,
it reappeared as unconcerned as possible.   It is a
song-bird, a thrush, and gives a feature to these
mountain streams and waterfalls which ours, except
on the Pacific coast, entirely lack.   The stream
that winds through Grasmere vale, and flows against
the embankment of the churchyard, as the Avon at
Stratford, is of great beauty, — clean, bright, full,
trouty, with just a tinge of gypsy blood in its veins,
which it gets from the black tarns on the mountains, and which adds to its richness of color.   I
saw an angler take a few trout from it, in a meadow
near the village.   After a heavy rain the stream
was not roily, but slightly darker in hue; these
fields and mountains are so turf-bound that no particle of soil is carried away by the water.

Falls and cascades are a great feature all through this country, as they are a marked feature in Wordsworth's poetry. One's ear is everywhere haunted by the sound of falling water; and, when the ear cannot hear them, the eye can see the streaks or patches of white foam down the green declivities. There are no trees above the valley bottom to obstruct the view, and no hum of woods to muffle the sounds of distant streams. When I was at Grasmere there was much rain, and this stanza of the poet came to mind: —

> " Loud is the Vale! The voice is up
> With which she speaks when storms are gone,
> A mighty unison of streams!
> Of all her voices, one! "

The words "vale" and "dell" come to have a new meaning after one has visited Wordsworth's country, just as the words "cottage" and "shepherd" also have so much more significance there and in Scotland than at home.

> " Dear child of Nature, let them rail!
> — There is a nest in a green dale,
> A harbor and a hold,
> Where thou, a wife and friend, shalt see
> Thy own delightful days, and be
> A light to young and old."

Every humble dwelling looks like a nest; that in which the poet himself lived had a cozy, nest-like look; and every vale is green, — a cradle amid rocky heights, padded and carpeted with the thickest turf.

Wordsworth is described as the poet of nature. He is more the poet of man, deeply wrought upon

by a certain phase of nature, — the nature of those
sombre, quiet, green, far-reaching mountain solitudes. There is a shepherd quality about him; he
loves the flocks, the heights, the tarn, the tender
herbage, the sheltered dell, the fold, with a kind
of poetized shepherd instinct. Lambs and sheep
and their haunts, and those who tend them, recur
perpetually in his poems. How well his verse
harmonizes with those high, green, and gray solitudes, where the silence is broken only by the bleat
of lambs or sheep, or just stirred by the voice
of distant waterfalls! Simple, elemental yet pro-
foundly tender and human, he had

> "The primal sympathy
> Which, having been, must ever be."

He brooded upon nature, but it was nature mirrored
in his own heart. In his poem of "The Brothers"
he says of his hero, who had gone to sea: —

> "He had been rear'd
> Among the mountains, and he in his heart
> Was half a shepherd on the stormy seas.
> Oft in the piping shrouds had Leonard heard
> The tones of waterfalls, and inland sounds
> Of caves and trees;"

and, leaning over the vessel's side and gazing into
the "broad green wave and sparkling foam," he

> "Saw mountains, — saw the forms of sheep that grazed
> On verdant hills."

This was what his own heart told him; every experience or sentiment called those beloved images to
his own mind.

One afternoon, when the sun seemed likely to

get the better of the soft rain-clouds, I set out to
climb to the top of Helvellyn. I followed the
highway a mile or more beyond the Swan Inn, and
then I committed myself to a footpath that turns
up the mountain-side to the right, and crosses into
Grisedale and so to Ulleswater. Two schoolgirls
whom I overtook put me on the right track. The
voice of a foaming mountain torrent was in my ears
a long distance, and now and then the path crossed
it. Fairfield Mountain was on my right hand,
Helm Crag and Dunmail Raise on my left. Grasmere plain soon lay far below. The haymakers,
encouraged by a gleam of sunshine, were hastily
raking together the rain-blackened hay. From my
outlook they appeared to be slowly and laboriously
rolling up a great sheet of dark brown paper, un-
covering beneath it one of the most fresh and vivid
green. The mown grass is so long in curing in
this country (frequently two weeks) that the new
blades spring beneath it, and a second crop is well
under way before the old is "carried." The long
mountain slopes up which I was making my way
were as verdant as the plain below me. Large
coarse ferns or bracken, with an under-lining of fine
grass, covered the ground on the lower portions.
On the higher, grass alone prevailed. On the top
of the divide, looking down into the valley of
Ulleswater, I came upon one of those black tarns,
or mountain lakelets, which are such a feature in this
strange scenery. The word "tarn" has no meaning with us, though our young poets sometimes use

it as they do this Yorkshire word "wold;" one they get from Wordsworth, the other from Tennyson. But when you have seen one of those still, inky pools at the head of a silent, lonely Westmoreland dale, you will not be apt to misapply the word in future. Suddenly the serene shepherd mountain opens this black, gleaming eye at your feet, and it is all the more weird for having no eyebrow of rocks, or fringe of rush or bush. The steep, encircling slopes drop down and hem it about with the most green and uniform turf. If its rim had been modeled by human hands, it could not have been more regular or gentle in outline. Beneath its emerald coat the soil is black and peaty, which accounts for the hue of the water and the dark line that encircles it.

> " All round this pool both flocks and herds might drink
> On its firm margin, even as from a well,
> Or some stone basin, which the herdsman's hand
> Had shaped for their refreshment."

The path led across the outlet of the tarn, and then divided, one branch going down into the head of Grisedale, and the other mounting up the steep flank of Helvellyn. Far up the green acclivity I met a man and two young women making their way slowly down. They had come from Glenridding on Ulleswater, and were going to Grasmere. The women looked cold, and said I would find it wintry on the summit.

Helvellyn has a broad flank and a long back, and comes to a head very slowly and gently. You

reach a wire fence well up on the top that divides
some sheep ranges, pass through a gate, and have
a mile yet to the highest ground in front of you;
but you could traverse it in a buggy, it is so smooth
and grassy. The grass fails just before the summit
is reached, and the ground is covered with small
fragments of the decomposed rock. The view is
impressive, and such as one likes to sit down to
and drink in slowly, — a

> "Grand terraqueous spectacle,
> From centre to circumference, unveil'd."

The wind was moderate and not cold. Toward
Ulleswater the mountain drops down abruptly many
hundred feet, but its vast western slope appeared
one smooth, unbroken surface of grass. The following jottings in my notebook, on the spot, preserve some of the features of the scene: "All the
northern landscape lies in the sunlight as far as
Carlisle,

> 'A tumultuous waste of huge hilltops;'

not quite so severe and rugged as the Scotch mountains, but the view more pleasing and more exten-
sive than the one I got from Ben Venue. The
black tarns at my feet, — Keppel Cove Tarn one of
them, according to my map, — how curious they
look! I can just discern the figure of a man moving by the marge of one of them. Away beyond
Ulleswater is a vast sweep of country flecked here
and there by slowly moving cloud shadows. To
the northeast, in places, the backs and sides of the
mountains have a green, pastoral voluptuousness, so

smooth and full are they with thick turf. At other
points the rock has fretted through the verdant
carpet. St. Sunday's Crag to the west, across
Grisedale, is a steep acclivity covered with small,
loose stones, as if they had been dumped over the
top, and were slowly sliding down; but nowhere
do I see great bowlders strewn about. Patches of
black peat are here and there. The little rills, near
and far, are white as milk, so swiftly do they run.
On the more precipitous sides the grass and moss
are lodged, and hold like snow, and are as tender
in hue as the first April blades. A multitude of
lakes are in view, and Morecambe Bay to the south.
There are sheep everywhere, loosely scattered, with
their lambs; occasionally I hear them bleat. No
other sound is heard but the chirp of the mountain
pipit. I see the wheat-ear flitting here and there.
One mountain now lies in full sunshine, as fat as
a seal, wrinkled and dimpled where it turns to
the west, like a fat animal when it bends to lick
itself. What a spectacle is now before me! — all
the near mountains in shadow, and the distant in
strong sunlight; I shall not see the like of that
again. On some of the mountains the green vestments are in tatters and rags, so to speak, and
barely cling to them. No heather in view. Toward Windermere the high peaks and crests are much
more jagged and rocky. The air is filled with the
same white, motionless vapor as in Scotland. When
the sun breaks through, —

> 'Slant watery lights, from parting clouds, apace
> Travel along the precipice's base,
> Cheering its naked waste of scatter'd stone.' "

Amid these scenes one comes face to face with nature,

> " With the pristine earth,
> The planet in its nakedness,"

as he cannot in a wooded country. The primal, abysmal energies, grown tender and meditative, as it were, thoughtful of the shepherd and his flocks, and voiceful only in the leaping torrents, look out upon one near at hand and pass a mute recognition. Wordsworth perpetually refers to these hills and dales as lonely or lonesome; but his heart was still more lonely. The outward solitude was congenial to the isolation and profound privacy of his own soul. "Lonesome," he says of one of these mountain dales, but

> "Not melancholy, — no, for it is green
> And bright and fertile, furnished in itself
> With the few needful things that life requires.
> In rugged arms how soft it seems to lie,
> How tenderly protected."

It is this tender and sheltering character of the mountains of the Lake district that is one main source of their charm. So rugged and lofty, and yet so mellow and delicate! No shaggy, weedy growths or tangles anywhere; nothing wilder than the bracken, which at a distance looks as solid as the grass. The turf is as fine and thick as that of a lawn. The dainty-nosed lambs could not crave a tenderer bite than it affords. The wool of the dams could hardly be softer to the foot. The last of July the grass was still short and thick, as if it never shot up a stalk and produced seed, but always remained a fine, close mat. Nothing was more unlike what I was used to at home than this universal tendency (the same is true in Scotland and in Wales) to grass, and, on the lower slopes, to bracken, as if these were the only two plants in nature. Many of these eminences in the north of England, too lofty for hills and too smooth for mountains, are called fells. The railway between Carlisle and Preston winds between them, as Houghill Fells, Tebay Fells, Shap Fells, etc. They are, even in midsummer, of such a vivid and uniform green that it seems as if they must have been painted. Nothing blurs or mars the hue; no stalk of weed or stem of dry grass. The scene, in singleness and purity of tint, rivals the blue of the sky. Nature does not seem to ripen and grow sere as autumn approaches, but wears the tints of May in October.

VIII

A GLANCE AT BRITISH WILD FLOWERS

THE first flower I plucked in Britain was the daisy, in one of the parks in Glasgow. The sward had recently been mown, but the daisies dotted it as thickly as stars. It is a flower almost as common as the grass; find a square foot of green-sward anywhere, and you are pretty sure to find a daisy, probably several of them. Bairnwort — child's flower — it is called in some parts, and its expression is truly infantile. It is the favorite of all the poets, and when one comes to see it he does not think it has been a bit overpraised. Some flowers please us by their intrinsic beauty of color and form; others by their expression of certain human qualities: the daisy has a modest, lowly, un-obtrusive look that is very taking. A little white ring, its margin unevenly touched with crimson, it looks up at one like the eye of a child.

> "Thou unassuming Commonplace
> Of Nature, with that homely face,
> And yet with something of a grace,
> Which Love makes for thee!"

Not a little of its charm to an American is the unexpected contrast it presents with the rank, coarse ox-eye daisy so common in this country, and more or less abundant in Britain, too. The Scotch call this latter "dog daisy." I thought it even coarser, and taller there than with us. Though the commonest of weeds, the "wee, modest, crimson-tippit flower" sticks close at home; it seems to have none of the wandering, devil-may-care, vagabond propensities of so many other weeds. I believe it has never yet appeared upon our shores in a wild state, though Wordsworth addressed it thus: —

> " Thou wander'st this wild world about
> Unchecked by pride or scrupulous doubt."

The daisy is prettier in the bud than in the flower, as it then shows more crimson. It shuts up on the approach of foul weather; hence Tennyson says the daisy closes

> " Her crimson fringes to the shower."

At Alloway, whither I flitted from Glasgow, I first put my hand into the British nettle, and, I may add, took it out again as quickly as if I had put it into the fire. I little suspected that rank dark-green weed there amid the grass under the old apple-trees, where the blue speedwell and cockscombs grew, to be a nettle. But I soon learned that the one plant you can count on everywhere in England and Scotland is the nettle. It is the royal weed of Britain. It stands guard along every roadbank and hedge-row in the island.

Put your hand to the ground after dark in any fence corner, or under any hedge, or on the border of any field, and the chances are ten to one you will

take it back again with surprising alacrity. And
such a villainous fang as the plant has! it is like
the sting of bees. Your hand burns and smarts for
hours afterward. My little boy and I were eagerly
gathering wild flowers on the banks of the Doon,
when I heard him scream, a few yards from me.
I had that moment jerked my stinging hand out of
the grass as if I had put it into a hornet's nest, and
I knew what the youngster had found. We held
our burning fingers in the water, which only aggra-
vated the poison. It is a dark green, rankly growing plant, from one to two feet high, that asks no
leave of anybody. It is the police that protects
every flower in the hedge. To "pluck the flower
of safety from the nettle danger" is a figure of
speech that has especial force in this island. The
species of our own nettle with which I am best
acquainted, the large-leaved Canada nettle, grows
in the woods, is shy and delicate, is cropped by
cattle, and its sting is mild. But apparently no
cow's tongue can stand the British nettle, though,
when cured as hay, it is said to make good fodder.
Even the pigs cannot eat it till it is boiled. In
starvation times it is extensively used as a pot-herb,
and, when dried, its fibre is said to be nearly equal
to that of flax. Rough handling, I am told, dis-
arms it, but I could not summon up courage to try
the experiment. Ophelia made her garlands

"Of crow-flowers, daisies, nettles, and long purples."

But the nettle here referred to was probably the
stingless dead-nettle.

A Scotch farmer, with whom I became acquainted, took me on a Sunday afternoon stroll through his fields. I went to his kirk in the forenoon; in the afternoon he and his son went to mine, and liked the sermon as well as I did. These banks and braes of Doon, of a bright day in May, are eloquent enough for anybody. Our path led along the river course for some distance. The globe-flower, like a large buttercup with the petals partly closed, nodded here and there. On a broad, sloping, semicircular bank, where a level expanse of rich fields dropped down to a springy, rushy bottom near the river's edge, and which the Scotch call a brae, we reclined upon the grass and listened to the birds, all but the lark new to me, and discussed the flowers growing about. In a wet place the "gillyflower" was growing, suggesting our dentaria, or crinkle-root. This is said to be "the lady's smock all silver-white" of Shakespeare, but these were not white, rather a pale lilac. Near by, upon the ground, was the nest of the meadow pipit, a species of titlark, which my friend would have me believe was the wood-lark, — a bird I was on the lookout for. The nest contained six brown-speckled eggs, — a large number, I thought. But I found that this is the country in which to see birds'-nests crowded with eggs, as well as human habitations thronged with children. A white umbelliferous plant, very much like wild carrot, dotted the turf here and there. This, my companion said, was **pig**-nut, or ground-chestnut, and that there was a sweet, edible tuber at the root of it, and, to make his words good, dug up one with his fingers, recalling Caliban's words in the "Tempest": —

"And I, with my long nails, will dig thee pig-nuts."

The plant grows freely about England, but does not seem to be troublesome as a weed.

In a wooded slope beyond the brae, I plucked my first woodruff, a little cluster of pure white flowers, much like that of our saxifrage, with a delicate perfume. Its stalk has a whorl of leaves like the galium. As the plant dries its perfume increases, and a handful of it will scent a room.

The wild hyacinths, or bluebells, had begun to fade, but a few could yet be gathered here and there in the woods and in the edges of the fields. This is one of the plants of which nature is very prodigal in Britain. In places it makes the underwoods as blue as the sky, and its rank perfume loads the air. Tennyson speaks of "sheets of hyacinths." We have no wood flower in the Eastern States that grows in such profusion.

Our flowers, like our birds and wild creatures, are more shy and retiring than the British. They keep more to the woods, and are not sowed so broadcast. Herb Robert is exclusively a wood plant with us, but in England it strays quite out into the open fields and by the roadside. Indeed, in England I found no so-called wood flower that could not be met with more or less in the fields and along the hedges. The main reason, perhaps, is that the need of shelter is never so great there, neither winter nor summer, as it is here, and the supply of moisture is more uniform and abundant. In dampness, coolness, and shadiness, the whole climate is woodsy, while the atmosphere of the woods themselves is almost subterranean in its dankness and chilliness. The plants come out for sun and warmth, and every seed they scatter in this moist and fruitful soil takes.

How many exclusive wood flowers we have, most of our choicest kinds being of sylvan birth, — flowers that seem to vanish before the mere breath of cultivated fields, as wild as the partridge and the beaver, like the yellow violet, the arbutus, the medeola, the dicentra, the claytonia, the trilliums, many of the orchids, uvularia, dalibarda, and others. In England, probably, all these plants, if they grew there, would come out into the fields and opens. The wild strawberry, however, reverses this rule; it is more a wood plant in England than with us. Excepting the rarer variety (*Fragaria vesca*), our strawberry thrives best in cultivated fields, and Shakespeare's reference to this fruit would not be apt, —

> "The strawberry grows underneath the nettle;
> And wholesome berries thrive and ripen best,
> Neighbor'd by fruit of baser quality."

The British strawberry is found exclusively, I believe, in woods and copses, and the ripened fruit is smaller or lighter colored than our own.

Nature in this island is less versatile than with us, but more constant and uniform, less variety and

contrast in her works, and less capriciousness and
reservation also. She is chary of new species, but
multiplies the old ones endlessly. I did not observe so many varieties of wild flowers as at home,
but a great profusion of specimens; her lap is fuller,
but the kinds are fewer. Where you find one of
a kind, you will find ten thousand. Wordsworth
saw "golden daffodils,"

> " Continuous as the stars that shine
> And twinkle on the milky way,"

and one sees nearly all the common wild flowers in
the same profusion. The buttercup, the dandelion,
the ox-eye daisy, and other field flowers that have
come to us from Europe, are samples of how lav-
ishly Nature bestows her floral gifts upon the Old
World. In July the scarlet poppies are thickly
sprinkled over nearly every wheat and oat field in
the kingdom. The green waving grain seems to
have been spattered with blood. Other flowers
were alike universal. Not a plant but seems to
have sown itself from one end of the island to the
other. Never before did I see so much white
clover. From the first to the last of July, the
fields in Scotland and England were white with it.
Every square inch of ground had its clover blossom.
Such a harvest as there was for the honey-bee, unless the nectar was too much diluted with water in
this rainy climate, which was probably the case.
In traveling south from Scotland, the foxglove
traveled as fast as I did, and I found it just as
abundant in the southern counties as in the north-

ern. This is the most beautiful and conspicuous of all the wild flowers I saw, — a spire of large purple bells rising above the ferns and copses and along the hedges everywhere. Among the copses of Surrey and Hants, I saw it five feet high, and amid the rocks of North Wales still higher. We have no conspicuous wild flower that compares with it. It is so showy and abundant that the traveler on the express train cannot miss it; while the pedestrian finds it lining his way like rows of torches. The bloom creeps up the stalk gradually as the season advances, taking from a month to six weeks to go from the bottom to the top, making at all times a most pleasing gradation of color, and showing the plant each day with new flowers and a fresh, new look. It never looks shabby and spent, from first to last. The lower buds open the first week in June, and slowly the purple wave creeps upward; bell after bell swings to the bee and moth, till the end of July, when you see the stalk waving in the wind with two or three flowers at the top, as perfect and vivid as those that opened first. I wonder the poets have not mentioned it oftener. Tennyson speaks of "the foxglove spire." I note this allusion in Keats: —

> "Where the deer's swift leap
> Startles the wild bee from the fox-glove bell,"

and this from Coleridge: —

> "The fox-glove tall
> Sheds its loose purple bells or in the gust,
> Or when it bends beneath the upspringing lark,
> Or mountain finch alighting."

Coleridge perhaps knew that the lark did not perch
upon the stalk of the foxglove, or upon any other
stalk or branch, being entirely a ground bird and
not a percher, but he would seem to imply that it
did, in these lines.

A London correspondent calls my attention to
these lines from Wordsworth, —

> "Bees that soar
> High as the highest peak of Furness Fells,
> Yet murmur by the hour in foxglove bells ;"

and adds: "Less poetical, but as graphic, was a
Devonshire woman's comparison of a dull preacher
to a 'Drummle drane in a pop;' Anglicè, A drone
in a foxglove, — called a pop from children amusing
themselves with popping its bells."

The prettiest of all humble roadside flowers I
saw was the little blue speedwell. I was seldom
out of sight of it anywhere in my walks till near
the end of June; while its little bands and assem-
blages of deep blue flowers in the grass by the roadside, turning a host of infantile faces up to the sun,
often made me pause and admire. It is prettier
than the violet, and larger and deeper colored than
our houstonia. It is a small and delicate edition
of our hepatica, done in indigo blue and wonted to
the grass in the fields and by the waysides.

> "The little speedwell's darling blue,"

sings Tennyson. I saw it blooming, with the daisy
and the buttercup, upon the grave of Carlyle. The
tender human and poetic element of this stern rocky
nature was well expressed by it.

In the Lake district I saw meadows purple with
a species of wild geranium, probably *Geranium
pratense*. It answered well to our wild geranium,
which in May sometimes covers wettish meadows
in the same manner, except that this English species
was of a dark blue purple. Prunella, I noticed,
was of a much deeper purple there than at home.
The purple orchids also were stronger colored, but
less graceful and pleasing, than our own. One
species which I noticed in June, with habits similar
to our purple fringed-orchis, perhaps the pyramidal
orchis, had quite a coarse, plebeian look. Probably
the most striking blue and purple wild flowers we
have are of European origin, as succory, blue-weed
or bugloss, vervain, purple loosestrife, and harebell.
These colors, except with the fall asters and gentians,
seem rather unstable in our flora.

It has been observed by the Norwegian botanist
Schübeler that plants and trees in the higher latitudes have larger leaves and larger flowers than
farther south, and that many flowers which are
white in the south become violet in the far north.
This agrees with my own observation. The feebler
light necessitates more leaf surface, and the fewer
insects necessitate larger and more showy flowers to
attract them and secure cross-fertilization. Blackberry blossoms, so white with us, are a decided
pink in England. The same is true of the water-
plantain. Our houstonia and hepatica would probably become a deep blue in that country. The
marine climate probably has something to do also

with this high color of the British flowers, as I
have noticed that on our New England coast the
same flowers are deeper tinted than they are in
the interior.

A flower which greets all ramblers to moist fields
and tranquil watercourses in midsummer is the
meadow-sweet, called also queen of the meadows.
It belongs to the Spiræa tribe, where our hardhack,
nine-bark, meadow-sweet, queen of the prairie, and
others belong, but surpasses all our species in being
sweet-scented, — a suggestion of almonds and cinnamon.   I saw much of it about Stratford, and in
rowing on the Avon plucked its large clusters of
fine, creamy white flowers from my boat.   Arnold
is felicitous in describing it as the "blond meadow-
sweet."

They cultivate a species of clover in England
that gives a striking effect to a field when in bloom,
Trifolium incarnatum, the long heads as red as
blood.   It is grown mostly for green fodder.   I
saw not one spear of timothy grass in all my rambles.   Though this is a grass of European origin,
yet it seems to be quite unknown among English
and Scotch farmers.   The horse bean, or Winchester bean, sown broadcast, is a new feature, while its
perfume, suggesting that of apple orchards, is the
most agreeable to be met with.

I was delighted with the furze, or whin, as the
Scotch call it, with its multitude of rich yellow,
pea-like blossoms exhaling a perfume that reminded
me of mingled cocoanut and peaches.   It is   a

prickly, disagreeable shrub to the touch, like our
ground juniper. It seems to mark everywhere the
line of cultivation; where the furze begins the plow
stops. It covers heaths and commons, and, with
the heather, gives that dark hue to the Scotch and
English uplands. The heather I did not see in all
its glory. It was just coming into bloom when I
left, the last of July; but the glimpses I had of it
in North Wales, and again in northern Ireland,
were most pleasing. It gave a purple border or
fringe to the dark rocks (the rocks are never so
lightly tinted in this island as ours are) that was
very rich and striking. The heather vies with the
grass in its extent and uniformity. Until midsummer it covers the moors and uplands as with a dark
brown coat. When it blooms, this coat becomes a
royal robe. The flower yields honey to the bee,
and the plant shelter to the birds and game, and is
used by the cottagers for thatching, and for twisting
into ropes, and for various other purposes.

Several troublesome weeds I noticed in England
that have not yet made their appearance in this
country. Coltsfoot invests the plowed lands there,
sending up its broad fuzzy leaves as soon as the
grain is up, and covering large areas. It is found
in this country, but, so far as I have observed, only
in out-of-the-way places.

Sheep sorrel has come to us from over seas, and
reddens many a poor worn-out field; but the larger
species of sorrel, *Rumex acetosa*, so common in
English fields, and shooting up a stem two feet

high, was quite new to me.   Nearly all the related
species, the various docks, are naturalized upon our
shores.

On the whole the place to see European weeds
is in America.   They run riot here.   They are like
boys out of school, leaping all bounds.   They have
the freedom of the whole broad land, and are allowed
to take possession in a way that would astonish a
British farmer.   The Scotch thistle is much rarer
in Scotland than in New York or Massachusetts.
I saw only one mullein by the roadside, and that
was in Wales, though it flourishes here and there
throughout the island.   The London correspondent,
already quoted, says of the mullein: "One will
come up in solitary glory, but, though it bears hundreds of flowers, many years will elapse before
another is seen in the same neighborhood.   We
used to say, 'There is a mullein coming up in such
a place,' much as if we had seen a comet; and its
flannel-like leaves and the growth of its spike were
duly watched and reported on day by day."   I did
not catch a glimpse of blue-weed, Bouncing Bet,
elecampane, live-for-ever, bladder campion, and others, of which I see acres at home, though all these
weeds do grow there.   They hunt the weeds mer-
cilessly; they have no room for them.   You see
men and boys, women and girls, in the meadows and
pastures cutting them out.   A species of wild mustard infests the best grain lands in June; when in
bloom it gives to the oat-fields a fresh canary yellow.   Then men and boys walk carefully through

the drilled grain and pull the mustard out, and
carry it away, leaving not one blossom visible.

On the whole, I should say that the British wild
flowers were less beautiful than our own, but more
abundant and noticeable, and more closely associated
with the country life of the people; just as their
birds are more familiar, abundant, and vociferous
than our songsters, but not so sweet-voiced and
plaintively melodious. An agreeable coarseness and
robustness characterize most of their flowers, and
they more than make up in abundance where they
lack in grace.

The surprising delicacy of our first spring flowers, of the hepatica, the spring beauty, the arbutus,
the bloodroot, the rue-anemone, the dicentra, — a
beauty and delicacy that pertains to exclusive wood
forms, — contrasts with the more hardy, hairy, hedge-
row look of their firstlings of the spring, like the
primrose, the hyacinth, the wood spurge, the green
hellebore, the hedge garlic, the moschatel, the
daffodil, the celandine, and others. Most of these
flowers take one by their multitude; the primrose
covers broad hedge banks for miles as with a carpet of bloom. In my excursions into field and
forest I saw nothing of the intense brilliancy of our
cardinal flower, which almost baffles the eye; nothing with the wild grace of our meadow or mountain lilies; no wood flower so taking to the eye as
our painted trillium and lady's-slipper; no bog
flower that compares with our calopogon and are-
thusa, so common in southeastern New England;

no brookside flower that equals our jewel-weed; no rock flower before which one would pause with the same feeling of admiration as before our columbine; no violet as striking as our bird's-foot violet; no trailing flower that approaches our matchless arbutus; no fern as delicate as our maiden-hair; no flowering shrub as sweet as our azaleas. In fact, their flora presented a commoner type of beauty, very comely and pleasing, but not so exquisite and surprising as our own. The contrast is well shown in the flowering of the maples of the two countries, — that of the European species being stiff and coarse compared with the fringe-like grace and delicacy of our maple. In like manner the silken tresses of our white pine contrast strongly with the coarser foliage of the European pines. But what they have, they have in greatest profusion. Few of their flowers waste their sweetness on the desert air; they throng the fields, lanes, and highways, and are known and seen of all. They bloom on the housetops, and wave from the summits of castle walls. The spring meadows are carpeted with flowers, and the midsummer grain-fields, from one end of the kingdom to the other, are spotted with fire and gold in the scarlet poppies and corn marigolds.

I plucked but one white pond-lily, and that was in the Kew Gardens, where I suppose the plucking was trespassing. Its petals were slightly blunter than ours, and it had no perfume. Indeed, in the matter of sweet-scented flowers, our flora shows by

far the more varieties, the British flora seeming
richer in this respect by reason of the abundance of
specimens of any given kind.

It is, indeed, a flowery land; a kind of perpetual
spring-time reigns there, a perennial freshness and
bloom such as our fierce skies do not permit.

IX

I

IN crossing the Atlantic from the New World to the Old, one of the first intimations the traveler has that he is nearing a strange shore, and an old and populous one, is the greater boldness and familiarity of the swarms of sea-gulls that begin to hover in the wake of the ship, and dive and contend with each other for the fragments and parings thrown overboard from the pantry. They have at once a different air and manner from those we left behind. How bold and tireless they are, pursuing the vessel from dawn to dark, and coming almost near enough to take the food out of your hand as you lean over the bulwarks. It is a sign in the air; it tells the whole story of the hungry and populous countries you are approaching; it is swarming and omnivorous Europe come out to meet you. You are near the sea-marge of a land teeming with life, a land where the prevailing forms are indeed few, but these on the most copious and vehement scale; where the birds and animals are not only more numerous than at home, but more dominating and aggressive, more closely associated with man, contending with him for the fruits of the soil, learned in his ways, full of resources, prolific, tenacious of life, not easily checked or driven out, — in fact, characterized by greater persistence and fecundity. This fact is sure, sooner or later, to strike the American in Britain. There seems to be an aboriginal push and heat in animate nature there, to behold which is a new experience. It is the Old World, and yet it really seems the New in the virility and hardihood of its species.

The New Englander who sees with evil forebodings the rapid falling off of the birth-rate in his own land, the family rills shrinking in these later generations, like his native streams in summer, and who consequently fears for the perpetuity of the race, may see something to comfort him in the British islands. Behold the fecundity of the parent stock! The drought that has fallen upon the older parts of the New World does not seem to have affected the sources of being in these islands. They are apparently as copious and exhaustless as they were three centuries ago. Britain might well appropriate to herself the last half of Emerson's quatrain: —

> " No numbers have counted my tallies,
>   No tribes my house can fill;
>   I sit by the shining Fount of Life,
>   And pour the deluge still."

For it is literally a deluge; the land is inundated with humanity. Thirty millions of people within the area of one of our larger States, and who shall

say that high-water mark is yet reached? Everything betokens a race still in its youth, still on the
road to empire. The full-bloodedness, the large
feet and hands, the prominent canine teeth, the
stomachic and muscular robustness, the health of
the women, the savage jealousy of personal rights,
the swarms upon swarms of children and young
people, the delight in the open air and in athletic
sports, the love of danger and adventure, a certain
morning freshness and youthfulness in their look,
as if their food and sleep nourished them well,
together with a certain animality and stupidity, —
all indicate a people who have not yet slackened
speed or taken in sail. Neither the land nor the
race shows any exhaustion. In both there is yet
the freshness and fruitfulness of a new country
You would think the people had just come int
possession of a virgin soil. There is a pioneer
hardiness and fertility about them. Families increase as in our early frontier settlements. Let me
quote a paragraph from Taine's "Notes:" —

"An Englishman nearly always has many children, — the rich as well as the poor. The Queen
has nine, and sets the example. Let us run over
the families we are acquainted with: Lord —— has
six children; the Marquis of ——, twelve; Sir
N——, nine; Mr. S——, a judge, twenty-four, of
whom twenty-two are living; several clergymen,
five, six, and up to ten and twelve."

Thus is the census kept up and increased. The
land, the towns and cities, are like hives in swarm-

ing time; a fertile queen indeed, and plenty of brood-comb! Were it not for the wildernesses of America, of Africa, and Australia, to which these swarms migrate, the people would suffocate and trample each other out. A Scotch or English city, compared with one of ours, is a kind of duplex or compound city; it has a double interior, — the interior of the closes and alleys, in which and out of which the people swarm like flies. Every country village has its closes, its streets between streets, where the humbler portion of the population is packed away. This back-door humanity streams forth to all parts of the world, and carries the national virtues with it. In walking through some of the older portions of Edinburgh, I was somehow reminded of colonies of cliff swallows I had seen at home, packed beneath the eaves of a farmer's barn, every inch of space occupied, the tenements crowding and lapping over each other, the interstices filled, every coign of vantage seized upon, the pendent beds and procreant cradles ranked one above another, and showing all manner of quaint and ingenious forms and adaptability to circumstances. In both London and Edinburgh there are streets above streets, or huge viaducts that carry one torrent of humanity above another torrent. They utilize the hills and depressions to make more surface room for their swarming myriads.

One day, in my walk through the Trosachs in the Highlands, I came upon a couple of ant-hills that arrested my attention. They were a type of

the country. They were not large, scarcely larger
than a peck measure, but never before had I seen
ant-hills so populous and so lively. They were
living masses of ants, while the ground for yards
about literally rustled with their numbers. I knew
ant-hills at home, and had noted them carefully,
hills that would fill a cart-box; but they were like
empty tenements compared with these, a fort gar-
risoned with a company instead of an army corps.
These hills stood in thin woods by the roadside.
From each of them radiated five main highways,
like the spokes of a wheel. These highways were
clearly defined to the eye, the grass and leaves
being slightly beaten down. Along each one of
them there was a double line of ants, — one line
going out for supplies and the other returning with
booty, — worms, flies, insects, a constant stream of
game going into the capitol. If the ants, with any
given worm or bug, got stuck, those passing out
would turn and lend a helping hand. The ground
between the main highways was being threaded in
all directions by individual ants, beating up and
down for game. The same was true of the surface
all about the terminus of the roads, several yards
distant. If I stood a few moments in one place,
the ants would begin to climb up my shoes and so
up my legs. Stamping them off seemed only to
alarm and enrage the whole camp, so that I would
presently be compelled to retreat. Seeing a big
straddling beetle, I caught him and dropped him
upon the nest. The ants attacked him as wolves

might attack an elephant. They clung to his legs,
they mounted his back, and assaulted him in front.
As he rushed through and over their ranks, down
the side of the mound, those clinging to his legs
were caught hold of by others, till lines of four or
five ants were being jerked along by each of his six
legs. The infuriated beetle cleared the mound,
and crawled under leaves and sticks to sweep off his
clinging enemies, and finally seemed to escape them
by burying himself in the earth. Then I took one
of those large, black, shelless snails with which this
land abounds, a snail the size of my thumb, and
dropped it upon the nest. The ants swarmed upon
it at once, and began to sink their jaws into it.
This woke the snail up to the true situation, and
it showed itself not without resources against its
enemies. Flee, like the beetle, it could not, but
it bore an invisible armor; it began to excrete from
every pore of its body a thick, whitish, viscid substance, that tied every ant that came in contact
with it, hand and foot, in a twinkling. When a
thick coating of this impromptu bird-lime had been
exuded, the snail wriggled right and left a few
times, partly sloughing it off, and thus ingulfing
hundreds of its antagonists. Never was army of
ants or of men bound in such a Stygian quagmire
before. New phalanxes rushed up and tried to
scale the mass; most of them were mired like their
fellows, but a few succeeded and gained the snail's
back; then began the preparation of another avalanche of glue; the creature seemed to dwindle in

size, and to nerve itself to the work; as fast as the ants reached him in any number he ingulfed them; he poured the vials of his glutinous wrath upon them till he had formed quite a rampart of cemented and helpless ants about him; fresh ones constantly coming up laid hold of the barricade with their jaws, and were often hung that way. I lingered half an hour or more to see the issue, but was finally compelled to come away before the closing scene. I presume the ants finally triumphed. The snail had nearly exhausted its ammunition; each new broadside took more and more time and was less and less effective; while the ants had unlimited resources, and could make bridges of their sunken armies. But how they finally freed themselves and their mound of that viscid, sloughing monster I should be glad to know.

But it was not these incidents that impressed me so much as the numbers and the animation of the ants, and their raiding, buccaneering propensities. When I came to London, I could not help thinking of the ant-hill I had seen in the North. This, I said, is the biggest ant-hill yet. See the great steam highways, leading to all points of the compass; see the myriads swarming, jostling each other in the streets, and overflowing all the surrounding country. See the underground tunnels and galleries and the overground viaducts; see the activity and the supplies, the whole earth the hunting-ground of these insects and rustling with their multitudinous stir. One may be pardoned, in the presence of such an enormous aggregate of humanity as London shows, for thinking of insects. Men and women seem cheapened and belittled, as if the spawn of blow-flies had turned to human beings. How the throng stream on interminably, the streets like river-beds, full to their banks! One hardly notes the units, — he sees only the black tide. He loses himself, and becomes an insignificant ant with the rest. He is borne along through the galleries and passages to the underground railway, and is swept forward like a drop in the sea. I used to make frequent trips to the country, or seek out some empty nook in St. Paul's, to come to my senses. But it requires no ordinary effort to find one's self in St. Paul's, and in the country you must walk fast or London will overtake you. When I would think I had a stretch of road all to myself, a troop of London bicyclists would steal up behind me and suddenly file by like spectres. The whole land is London-struck. You feel the suction of the huge city wherever you are. It draws like a cyclone; every current tends that way. It would seem as if cities and towns were constantly breaking from their moorings and drifting thitherward and joining themselves to it. On every side one finds smaller cities welded fast. It spreads like a malignant growth, that involves first one organ and then another. But it is not malignant. On the contrary, it is perhaps as normal and legitimate a city as there is on the globe. It is the proper outcome and expression of that fertile and bountiful land,

and that hardy, multiplying race. It seems less
the result of trade and commerce, and more the
result of the domestic home-seeking and home-build-
ing instinct, than any other city I have yet seen.
I felt, and yet feel, its attraction. It is such an
aggregate of actual human dwellings that this feeling pervades the very air. All its vast and multi-
plex industries, and its traffic, seem domestic, like
the chores about the household. I used to get
glimpses of it from the northwest borders, from
Hampstead Heath, and from about Highgate, lying
there in the broad, gentle valley of the Thames,
like an enormous country village — a village with
nearly four million souls, where people find life
sweet and wholesome, and keep a rustic freshness of
look and sobriety of manner. See their vast parks
and pleasure grounds; see the upper Thames, of a
bright Sunday, alive with rowing parties; see them
picnicking in all the country adjacent. Indeed, in
summer a social and even festive air broods over
the whole vast encampment. There is squalor and
misery enough, of course, and too much, but this
takes itself away to holes and corners.

II

A fertile race, a fertile nature, swarm in these
islands. The climate is a kind of prolonged May,
and a vernal lustiness and raciness are characteristic
of all the prevailing forms. Life is rank and full.
Reproduction is easy. There is plenty of sap,
plenty of blood. The salt of the sea prickles in

the veins; the spawning waters have imparted their virility to the land. 'T is a tropical and an arctic nature combined, the fruitfulness of one and the activity of the other.

The national poet is Shakespeare. In him we get the literary and artistic equivalents of this teeming, racy, juicy land and people. It needs just such a soil, just such a background, to account for him. The poetic value of this continence on the one hand, and of this riot and prodigality on the other, is in his pages.

The teeming human populations reflect only the general law: there is the same fullness of life in the lower types, the same push and hardiness. It is the opinion of naturalists that the prevailing European forms are a later production than those of the southern hemisphere or of the United States, and hence, according to Darwin's law, should be more versatile and dominating. That this last fact holds good with regard to them, no competent observer can fail to see. When European plants and animals come into competition with American, the latter, for the most part, go to the wall, as do the natives in Australia. Or shall we say that the native species flee before the advent of civilization, the denuding the land of its forests, and the European species come in and take their place? Yet the fact remains, that that trait or tendency to persist in the face of obstacles, to hang on by tooth and nail, ready in new expedients, thriving where others starve, climbing where others fall, multiply-

ing where others perish, like certain weeds, which
if you check the seed, will increase at the root, is
more marked in the forms that have come to us
from Europe than in the native inhabitants. Nearly
everything that has come to this country from the
Old World has come prepared to fight its way
through and take possession. The European or
Old World man, the Old World animals, the Old
World grasses and grains, and weeds and vermin,
are in possession of the land, and the native species
have given way before them. The honey-bee, with
its greed, its industry, and its swarms, is a fair
type of the rest. The English house sparrow,
which we were at such pains to introduce, breeds
like vermin and threatens to become a plague in the
land. Nearly all our troublesome weeds are European. When a new species gets a foothold here,
it spreads like fire. The European rats and mice
would eat us up, were it not for the European cats
we breed. The wolf not only keeps a foothold in
old and populous countries like France and Germany, but in the former country has so increased
of late years that the government has offered an
additional bounty upon their pelts. When has an
American wolf been seen or heard in our comparatively sparsely settled Eastern or Middle States?
They have disappeared as completely as the beavers.
Yet is it probably true that, in a new country like
ours, a tendency slowly develops itself among the
wild creatures to return and repossess the land
under the altered conditions. It is so with the

plants, and probably so with the animals. Thus, the chimney swallows give up the hollow trees for the chimneys, the cliff swallows desert the cliffs for the eaves of the barns, the squirrels find they can live in and about the fields, etc. In my own locality, our native mice are becoming much more numerous about the buildings than formerly; in the older settled portions of the country, the flying squirrel often breeds in the houses; the wolf does not seem to let go in the West as readily as he did in the East; the black bear is coming back to parts of the country where it had not been seen for thirty years.

I noticed many traits among the British animals and birds that looked like the result both of the sharp competition going on among themselves in their crowded ranks and of association with man. Thus, the partridge not only covers her nest, but carefully arranges the grass about it so that no mark of her track to and fro can be seen. The field mouse lays up a store of grain in its den in the ground, and then stops up the entrance from within. The woodcock, when disturbed, flies away with one of her young snatched up between her legs, and returns for another and another. The sea-gulls devour the grain in the fields; the wild ducks feed upon the oats; the crows and jackdaws pull up the sprouts of the newly-planted potatoes; the grouse, partridges, pigeons, fieldfares, etc., attack the turnips; the hawk frequently snatches the wounded game from under the gun of the sportsman; the crows perch upon the tops of the chimneys of the houses; in the East the stork builds upon the house-tops, in the midst of cities; in Scotland the rats follow the birds and the Highlanders to the herring fisheries along the coast, and disperse with them when the season is over; the eagle continues to breed in the mountains with the prize of a guinea upon every egg; the rabbits have to be kept down with nets and ferrets; the game birds — grouse, partridges, ducks, geese — continue to swarm in the face of the most inveterate race of sportsmen under the sun, and in a country where it is said the crows destroy more game than all the guns in the king-dom.

Many of the wild birds, when incubating, will allow themselves to be touched by the hand. The fox frequently passes the day under some covered drain or under some shelving bank near the farm buildings. The otter, which so long ago disap-peared from our streams, still holds its own in Scot-land, though trapped and shot on all occasions. A mother otter has been known boldly to confront a man carrying off her young.

Thomas Edward, the shoemaker-naturalist of Ab-erdeen, relates many adventures he had during his nocturnal explorations with weasels, polecats, badg-ers, owls, rats, etc., in which these creatures showed astonishing boldness and audacity. On one occasion, a weasel actually attacked him; on an-other, a polecat made repeated attempts to take a moor-hen from the breast pocket of his coat while he was trying to sleep. On still another occasion, while he was taking a nap, an owl robbed him of a mouse which he wished to take home alive, and which was tied by a string to his waistcoat. He says he has put his walking stick into the mouth of a fox just roused from his lair, and the fox worried the stick and took it away with him. Once, in descending a precipice, he cornered two foxes upon a shelf of rock, when the brutes growled at him and showed their teeth threateningly. As he let himself down to kick them out of his way, they bolted up the precipice over his person. Along the Scottish coast, crows break open shell-fish by carrying them high in the air and letting them drop upon the rocks. This is about as thoughtful a proceeding as that of certain birds of South Africa, which fly amid the clouds of migrating locusts and clip off the wings of the insects with their sharp beaks, causing them to fall to the ground, where they are devoured at leisure. Among the Highlands, the eagles live upon hares and young lambs; when the shepherds kill the eagles, the hares increase so fast that they eat up all the grass, and the flocks still suffer.

The scenes along the coast of Scotland during the herring-fishing, as described by Charles St. John in his "Natural History and Sport in Moray," are characteristic. The herrings appear in innumerable shoals, and are pursued by tens of thousands of birds in the air, and by the hosts of their enemies of the deep. Salmon and dog-fish prey upon them

from beneath; gulls, gannets, cormorants, and solan
geese prey upon them from above; while the fisher-
men from a vast fleet of boats scoop them up by
the million. The birds plunge and scream, the
men shout and labor, the sea is covered with broken
and wounded fish, the shore exhales the odor of the
decaying offal, which also attracts the birds and
the vermin; and, altogether, the scene is thoroughly
European. Yet the herring supply does not fail;
and when the shoals go into the lochs, the people
say they contain two parts fish to one of water.

One of the most significant facts I observed while
in England and Scotland was the number of eggs in
the birds'-nests. The first nest I saw, which was
that of the meadow pipit, held six eggs; the second, which was that of the willow warbler, contained seven. Are these British birds, then, I
said, like the people, really more prolific than our
own? Such is, undoubtedly, the fact. The nests
I had observed were not exceptional; and when a
boy told me he knew of a wren's nest with twenty-
six eggs in it, I was half inclined to believe him.
The common British wren, which is nearly identical with our winter wren, often does lay upward of
twenty eggs, while ours lays five or six. The long-
tailed titmouse lays from ten to twelve eggs; the
marsh tit, from eight to ten; the great tit, from six
to nine; the blue-bonnet, from six to eighteen; the
wryneck, often as many as ten; the nuthatch, seven;
the brown creeper, nine; the kinglet, eight; the
robin, seven; the flycatcher, eight; and so on, — all,

or nearly all, exceeding the number laid by corresponding species in this country. The highest
number of eggs of the majority of our birds is
five; some of the wrens and creepers and titmice
produce six, or even more; but as a rule one sees
only three or four eggs in the nests of our common
birds. Our quail seems to produce more eggs than
the European species, and our swift more.

Then this superabundance of eggs is protected by
such warm and compact nests. The nest of the
willow warbler, to which I have referred, is a kind
of thatched cottage upholstered with feathers. It
is placed upon the ground, and is dome-shaped, like
that of our meadow mouse, the entrance being on
the side. The chaffinch, the most abundant and
universal of the British birds, builds a nest in the
white thorn that is a marvel of compactness and
neatness. It is made mainly of fine moss and
wool. The nest of Jenny Wren, with its dozen
or more of eggs, is too perfect for art, and too
cunning for nature. Those I saw were placed amid
the roots of trees on a steep bank by the roadside.
You behold a mass of fine green moss set in an
irregular framework of roots, with a round hole in
the middle of it. As far in as your finger can
reach, it is exquisitely soft and delicately modeled.
When removed from its place, it is a large mass of
moss with the nest at the heart of it.

Then add to these things the comparative immu-
nity from the many dangers that beset the nests of
our birds, — dangers from squirrels, snakes, crows,

owls, weasels, etc., and from violent storms and tempests, — and one can quickly see why the British birds so thrive and abound. There is a chaffinch for every tree, and a rook and a starling for every square rod of ground. I think there would be still more starlings if they could find places to build, but every available spot is occupied; every hole in a wall, or tower, or tree, or stump; every niche about the farm buildings; every throat of the grinning gargoyles about the old churches and cathedrals; every cranny in towers and steeples and castle parapet, and the mouth of every rain-spout and gutter in which they can find a lodgment.

The ruins of the old castles afford a harbor to many species, the most noticeable of which are sparrows, starlings, doves, and swallows. Rochester Castle, the main tower or citadel of which is yet in a good state of preservation, is one vast dove-cote. The woman in charge told me there were then about six hundred doves there. They whitened the air as they flew and circled about. From time to time they are killed off and sent to market. At sundown, after the doves had gone to roost, the swifts appeared, seeking out their crannies. For a few moments the air was dark with them.

Look also at the rooks. They follow the plowmen like chickens, picking up the grubs and worms; and chickens they are, sable farm fowls of a wider range. Young rooks are esteemed a great delicacy. The four-and-twenty blackbirds baked in a pie, and set before the king, of the nursery rhyme, were very likely four-and-twenty young rooks. Rook-pie is a national dish, and it would seem as if the young birds are slaughtered in sufficient numbers to exterminate the species in a few years. But they have to be kept under, like the rabbits; inasmuch as they do not emigrate, like the people. I had heard vaguely that our British cousins eschewed all pie except rook-pie, but I did not fully realize the fact till I saw them shooting the young birds and shipping them to market. A rookery in one's grove or shade-trees may be quite a source of profit. The young birds are killed just before they are able to fly, and when they first venture upon the outer rim of the nest or perch upon the near branches. I witnessed this chicken-killing in a rookery on the banks of the Doon. The ruins of an old castle crowned the height overgrown with forest trees. In these trees the rooks nested, much after the fashion of our wild pigeons. A young man with a rifle was having a little sport by shooting the young rooks for the gamekeeper. There appeared to be fewer than a hundred nests, and yet I was told that as many as thirty dozen young rooks had been shot there that season. During the firing the parent birds circle high aloft, uttering their distressed cries. Apparently, no attempt is made to conceal the nests; they are placed far out upon the branches, several close together, showing as large dense masses of sticks and twigs. Year after year the young are killed, and yet the rookery is not abandoned, nor the old birds discouraged. It is to be added that this species is not the carrion crow, like ours, though so closely resembling it in appearance. It picks up its subsistence about the fields, and is not considered an unclean bird. The British carrion crow is a much more rare species. It is a strong, fierce bird, and often attacks and kills young lambs or rabbits.

What is true of the birds is true of the rabbits, and probably of the other smaller animals. The British rabbit breeds seven times a year, and usually produces eight young at a litter; while, so far as I have observed, the corresponding species in this country breeds not more than twice, producing from three to four young. The western gray rabbit is said to produce three or four broods a year of four to six young. It is calculated that in England a pair of rabbits will, in the course of four years, multiply to one million two hundred and fifty thousand. If unchecked for one season, this game would eat the farmers up. In the parks of the Duke of Hamilton, the rabbits were so numerous that I think one might have fired a gun at random with his eyes closed and knocked them over. They scampered right and left as I advanced, like leaves blown by the wind. Their cotton tails twinkled thicker than fireflies in our summer night. In the Highlands, where there were cultivated lands, and in various other parts of England and Scotland that I visited, they were more abundant than chipmunks in our beechen woods. The revenue derived from the sale of the ground game on some estates is an

important item. The rabbits are slaughtered in untold numbers throughout the island. They shoot
them, and hunt them with ferrets, and catch them
in nets and gins and snares, and they are the principal game of the poacher, and yet the land is alive
with them. Thirty million skins are used up annually in Great Britain, besides several million hare
skins. The fur is used for stuffing beds, and is
also made into yarn and cloth.

But the Colorado beetle is our own, and it shows
many of the European virtues. It is sufficiently
prolific and persistent to satisfy any standard; but
we cannot claim all the qualities for it till it has
crossed the Atlantic and established itself on the
other side.

There are other forms of life in which we surpass
the mother country. I did not hear the voice of
frog or toad while I was in England. Their marshes
were silent; their summer nights were voiceless.
I longed for the multitudinous chorus of my own
bog; for the tiny silver bells of our hylas, the long-
drawn and soothing *tr-r-r-r-r* of our twilight toads,
and the rattling drums, kettle and bass, of our pond
frogs. Their insect world, too, is far behind ours;
no fiddling grasshoppers, no purring tree-crickets,
no scraping katydids, no whirring cicadas; no sounds
from any of these sources by meadow or grove, by
night or day, that I could ever hear. We have a
large orchestra of insect musicians, ranging from
that tiny performer that picks the strings of his
instrument so daintily in the summer twilight, to

the shrill and piercing crescendo of the harvest-fly.
A young Englishman who had traveled over this
country told me he thought we had the noisiest
nature in the world. English midsummer nature
is the other extreme of stillness. The long twilight
is unbroken by a sound, unless in places by the
"clanging rookery." The British bumblebee, a
hairy, short-waisted fellow, has the same soft, mellow bass as our native bee, and his habits appear
much the same, except that he can stand the cold
and the wet much better (I used to see them very
lively after sundown, when I was shivering with
my overcoat on), and digs his own hole like the
rabbit, which ours does not. Sitting in the woods
one day, a bumblebee alighted near me on the
ground, and, scraping away the surface mould,
began to bite and dig his way into the earth, — a
true Britisher, able to dig his own hole.

In the matter of squirrel life, too, we are far
ahead of England. I believe there are more red
squirrels, to say nothing of gray squirrels, flying
squirrels, and chipmunks, within half a mile of my
house than in any county in England. In all my
loitering and prying about the woods and groves
there, I saw but two squirrels. The species is larger
than ours, longer and softer furred, and appears to
have little of the snickering, frisking, attitudinizing
manner of the American species. But England is
the paradise of snails. The trail of the snail is
over all. I have counted a dozen on the bole of a
single tree. I have seen them hanging to the

bushes and hedges like fruit. I heard a lady complain that they got into the kitchen, crawling about by night and hiding by day, and baffling her efforts to rid herself of them. The thrushes eat them, breaking their shells upon a stone. They are said to be at times a serious pest in the garden, devouring the young plants at night. When did the American snail devour anything, except, perhaps, now and then a strawberry? The bird or other creature that feeds on the large black snail of Britain, if such there be, need never go hungry, for I saw these snails even on the tops of mountains.

The same opulence of life that characterizes the animal world in England characterizes the vegetable. I was especially struck, not so much with the variety of wild flowers, as with their numbers and wide distribution. The ox-eye daisy and the buttercup are good samples of the fecundity of most European plants. The foxglove, the corn-poppy, the speedwell, the wild hyacinth, the primrose, the various vetches, and others grow in nearly the same profusion. The forget-me-not is very common, and the little daisy is nearly as universal as the grass. Indeed, as I have already stated in another chapter, nearly all the British wild flowers seemed to grow in the open manner and in the same abundance as our goldenrods and purple asters. They show no shyness, no wildness. Nature is not stingy of them, but fills her lap with each in its turn. Rare and delicate plants, like our arbutus, certain of our orchids and violets that hide in the woods and are

very fastidious and restricted in their range, probably have no parallel in England. The island is
small, is well assorted and compacted, and is thoroughly homogeneous in its soil and climate; the
conditions of field and forest and stream that exist
have long existed; a settled permanence and equipoise prevail; every creature has found its place,
every plant its home. There are no new experi-
ments to be made, no new risks to be run; life in
all its forms is established, and its current main-
tains a steady strength and fullness that an observer
from our spasmodic hemisphere is sure to appreciate.

X

A SUNDAY IN CHEYNE ROW

I

WHILE in London I took a bright Sunday afternoon to visit Chelsea, and walk along Cheyne Row and look upon the house in which Carlyle passed nearly fifty years of his life, and in which he died. Many times I paced to and fro. I had been there eleven years before, but it was on a dark, rainy night, and I had brought away no image of the street or house. The place now had a more humble and neglected look than I expected to see; nothing that suggested it had ever been the abode of the foremost literary man of his time, but rather the home of plain, obscure persons of little means. One would have thought that the long residence there of such a man as Carlyle would have enhanced the value of real estate for many squares around, and drawn men of wealth and genius to that part of the city. The Carlyle house was unoccupied, and, with its closed shutters and little pools of black sooty water standing in the brick area in front of the basement windows, looked dead and deserted indeed. But the house itself, though nearly two hundred years old, showed no signs of decay. It had doubtless witnessed the extinction of many households before that of the Carlyles.

My own visit to that house was in one autumn night in 1871. Carlyle was then seventy-six years old, his wife had been dead five years, his work was done, and his days were pitifully sad. He was out taking his after-dinner walk when we arrived, Mr. Conway and I; most of his walking and riding, it seems, was done after dark, an indication in itself of the haggard and melancholy frame of mind habitual to him. He presently appeared, wrapped in a long gray coat that fell nearly to the floor. His greeting was quiet and grandfatherly, and that of a man burdened with his own sad thoughts. I shall never forget the impression his large, long, soft hand made in mine, nor the look of sorrow and suffering stamped upon the upper part of the face, — sorrow mingled with yearning compassion. The eyes were bleared and filmy with unshed and unshedable tears. In pleasing contrast to his coarse hair and stiff, bristly, iron-gray beard, was the fresh, delicate color that just touched his brown cheeks, like the tinge of poetry that plays over his own rugged page. I noted a certain shyness and delicacy, too, in his manner, which contrasted in the same way with what is alleged of his rudeness and severity. He leaned his head upon his hand, the fingers thrust up through the hair, and, with his elbow resting upon the table, looked across to my companion, who kept the conversation going. This attitude he hardly changed during the two hours we sat there. How serious and concerned he looked, and how surprising that hearty, soliloquizing sort of laugh which now and then came from him as he talked, not so much a laugh provoked by anything humorous in the conversation, as a sort of foil to his thoughts, as one might say, after a severe judgment, "Ah, well-a-day, what matters it!" If that laugh could have been put in his Latter-day Pamphlets, where it would naturally come, or in his later political tracts, these publications would have given much less offense. But there was amusement in his laugh when I told him we had introduced the English sparrow in America. "Introduced!" he repeated, and laughed again. He spoke of the bird as a "comical little wretch," and feared we should regret the "introduction." He repeated an Arab proverb which says Solomon's Temple was built amid the chirping of ten thousand sparrows, and applied it very humorously in the course of his talk to the human sparrows that always stand ready to chirrup and cackle down every great undertaking. He had seen a cat walk slowly along the top of a fence while a row of sparrows seated upon a ridge-board near by all pointed at her and chattered and scolded, and by unanimous vote pronounced her this and that, but the cat went on her way all the same. The verdict of majorities was not always very formidable, however unanimous.

A monument had recently been erected to Scott in Edinburgh, and he had been asked to take part in some attendant ceremony. But he had refused peremptorily. "If the angel Gabriel had summoned me I would not have gone," he said. It was too soon to erect a monument to Scott. Let them wait a hundred years and see how they feel about it then. He had never met Scott: the nearest he had come to it was once when he was the bearer of a message to him from Goethe; he had rung at his door with some trepidation, and was relieved when told that the great man was out. Not long afterwards he had a glimpse of him while standing in the streets of Edinburgh. He saw a large wagon coming drawn by several horses, and containing a great many people, and there in the midst of them, full of talk and hilarity like a great boy, sat Scott. Carlyle had recently returned from his annual visit to Scotland, and was full of sad and tender memories of his native land. He was a man in whom every beautiful thing awakened melancholy thoughts. He spoke of the blooming lasses and the crowds of young people he had seen on the streets of some northern city, Aberdeen, I think, as having filled him with sadness; a kind of homesickness of the soul was upon him, and deepened with age, — a solitary and a bereaved man from first to last.

As I walked Cheyne Row that summer Sunday my eye rested again and again upon those three stone steps that led up to the humble door, each hollowed out by the attrition of the human foot, the middle one, where the force of the footfall would be greatest, most deeply worn of all, — worn by hundreds of famous feet, and many, many more

not famous. Nearly every notable literary man of
the century, both of England and America, had
trod those steps. Emerson's foot had left its mark
there, if one could have seen it, once in his prime
and again in his old age, and it was perhaps of him
I thought, and of his new-made grave there under
the pines at Concord, that summer afternoon as I
mused to and fro, more than of any other visitor to
that house. "Here we are shoveled together again,"
said Carlyle from behind his wife, with a lamp high
in his hand, that October night thirty-seven years
ago, as Jane opened the door to Emerson. The
friendship, the love of those two men for each
other, as revealed in their published correspondence,
is one of the most beautiful episodes in English
literary history. The correspondence was opened
and invited by Emerson, but as years went by it is
plain that it became more and more a need and a
solace to Carlyle. There is something quite pathetic
in the way he clung to Emerson and entreated him
for a fuller and more frequent evidence of his love.
The New Englander, in some ways, appears stinted
and narrow beside him; Carlyle was much the more
loving and emotional man. He had less self-com-
placency than Emerson, was much less stoical, and
felt himself much more alone in the world. Emerson was genial and benevolent from temperament
and habit; Carlyle was wrathful and vituperative,
while his heart was really bursting with sympathy
and love. The savagest man, probably, in the
world in his time, who had anything like his enor-

mous fund of tenderness and magnanimity. He was full of contempt for the mass of mankind, but he was capable of loving particular men with a depth and an intensity that more than makes the account good. And let me say here that the saving feature about Carlyle's contempt, which is such a stumbling-block till one has come to understand it, is its perfect sincerity and inevitableness, and the real humility in which it has its root. He cannot help it; it is genuine, and has a kind of felicity. Then there is no malice or ill-will in it, but pity rather, and pity springs from love. We also know that he is always dominated by the inexorable conscience, and that the standard by which he tries men is the standard of absolute rectitude and worthiness. Contempt without love and humility begets a sneering, mocking, deriding habit of mind, which was far enough from Carlyle's sorrowing denunciations. "The quantity of sorrow he has, does it not mean withal the quantity of *sympathy* he has, the quantity of faculty and victory he shall yet have? 'Our sorrow is the inverted image of our nobleness.' The depth of our despair measures what capability, and height of claim we have, to hope." (Cromwell.) Emerson heard many responding voices, touched and won many hearts, but Carlyle was probably admired and feared more than he was loved, and love he needed and valued above all else. Hence his pathetic appeals to Emerson, the one man he felt sure of, the one voice that reached him and moved him among his contemporaries. He felt

Emerson's serenity and courage, and seemed to cling to, while he ridiculed, that New World hope that shone in him so brightly.

The ship that carries the most sail is most buffeted by the winds and storms. Carlyle carried more sail than Emerson did, and the very winds of the globe he confronted and opposed; the one great movement of the modern world, the democratic movement, the coming forward of the people in their own right, he assailed and ridiculed in a vocabulary the most copious and telling that was probably ever used, and with a concern and a seriousness most impressive.

Much as we love and revere Emerson, and immeasurable as his service has been, especially to the younger and more penetrating minds, I think it will not do at all to say, as one of our critics (Mr. Stedman) has lately said, that Emerson is as "far above Carlyle as the affairs of the soul and universe are above those of the contemporary or even the historic world." Above him he certainly was, in a thinner, colder air, but not in any sense that implies greater power or a farther range. His sympathies with the concrete world and his gripe upon it were far less than Carlyle's. He bore no such burden, he fought no such battle, as the latter did. His mass, his velocity, his penetrating power, are far less. A tranquil, high-sailing, fair-weather cloud is Emerson, and a massive, heavy-laden storm-cloud is Carlyle. Carlyle was never placidly sounding the azure depths like Emerson, but always pouring

and rolling earthward, with wind, thunder, rain
and hail.   He reaches up to the Emersonian altitudes, but seldom disports himself there; never loses
himself, as Emerson sometimes does; the absorption
takes place in the other direction; he descends to
actual affairs and events with fierce precipitation.
Carlyle's own verdict, written in his journal on
Emerson's second visit to him in 1848, was much
to the same effect, and, allowing for the Carlylean
exaggeration, was true.   He wrote that Emerson
differed as much from himself "as a gymnosophist
sitting idle on a flowery bank may do from a wearied
worker and wrestler passing that way with many of
his bones broken."

All men would choose Emerson's fate, Emerson's
history; how rare, how serene, how inspiring, how
beautiful, how fortunate!   But as between these
two friends, our verdict must be that Carlyle did
the more unique and difficult, the more heroic,
piece of work.   Whether the more valuable and
important or not, it is perhaps too early in the day
to say, but certainly the more difficult and masterful.   As an artist, using the term in the largest
sense, as the master-worker in, and shaper of, the
Concrete, he is immeasurably Emerson's superior.
Emerson's two words were truth and beauty, which
lie, as it were, in the same plane, and the passage
from one to the other is easy; it is smooth sailing.
Carlyle's two words were truth and duty, which lie
in quite different planes, and the passage between
which is steep and rough.   Hence the pain, the

struggle, the picturesque power.   Try to shape the
actual world of politics and human affairs according
to the ideal truth, and see if you keep your serenity.   There is a Niagara gulf between them that
must be bridged.   But what a gripe this man had
upon both shores, the real and the ideal!   The
quality of action, of tangible performance, that lies
in his works, is unique.   "He has not so much
written as spoken," and he has not so much spoken
as he has actually wrought.   He experienced, in
each of his books, the pain and the antagonism of
the man of action.   His mental mood and attitude
are the same; as is also his impatience of abstractions, of theories, of subtleties, of mere words.   Indeed, Carlyle was essentially a man of action, as he
himself seemed to think, driven by fate into literature.   He is as real and as earnest as Luther or
Cromwell, and his faults are the same in kind.   Not
the mere *saying* of a thing satisfies him as it does
Emerson; you must *do* it; bring order out of chaos,
make the dead alive, make the past present, in some
way make your fine sayings point to, or result in,
fact.   He says the Perennial lies always in the
Concrete.   Subtlety of intellect, which conducts
you, "not to new clearness, but to ever-new abstruse-
ness, wheel within wheel, depth under depth," has
no charms for him.   "My erudite friend, the astonishing intellect that occupies itself in splitting hairs,
and not in twisting some kind of cordage and effec-
tual draught-tackle to take the road with, is not to
me the most astonishing of intellects."

Emerson split no hairs, but he twisted very little cordage for the rough draught-horses of this world. He tells us to hitch our wagon to a star; and the star is without doubt a good steed, when once fairly caught and harnessed, but it takes an astronomer to catch it. The value of such counsel is not very tangible unless it awakes us to the fact that every power of both heaven and earth is friendly to a noble and courageous activity.

Carlyle was impatient of Emerson's fine-spun sentences and transcendental sleight-of-hand. Indeed, from a literary point of view, one of the most interesting phases of the published correspondence between these two notable men is the value which each unwittingly set upon his own methods and work. Each would have the other like himself.

Emerson wants Emersonian epigrams from Carlyle, and Carlyle wants Carlylean thunder from Emerson. Each was unconsciously his own ideal. The thing which a man's nature calls him to do, — what else so well worth doing? Certainly nothing else to him, — but to another? How surely each one of us would make our fellow over in our own image! Carlyle wants Emerson more practical, more concrete, more like himself in short. "The vile Pythons of this Mud-world do verily require to have sun-arrows shot into them, and red-hot pokers stuck through them, according to occasion;" do this as I am doing it, or trying to do it, and I shall like you better. It is well to know that nature will make good compost of the carcass of an Oliver Cromwell, and produce a cart-load of turnips from the same; but it is better to appreciate and make the most of the live Oliver himself. "A faculty is in you for a *sort* of speech which is itself *action*, an artistic sort. You *tell* us with piercing emphasis that man's soul is great; *show* us a great soul of a man, in some work symbolic of such; this is the seal of such a message, and you will feel by and by that you are called to do this. I long to see some concrete Thing, some Event, Man's Hope, American Forest, or piece of Creation, which this Emerson loves and wonders at, well *Emersonized*, depicted by Emerson, filled with the life of Emerson and cast forth from him, then to live by itself." Again: "I will have all things condense themselves, take shape and body, if they are to have my sympathy; I have a *body* myself; in the brown leaf, sport of the Autumn winds, I find what mocks all prophesyings, even Hebrew ones." "Alas, it is so easy to screw one's self up into high and even higher altitudes of Transcendentalism, and see nothing under one but the everlasting snows of Himmalayah, the Earth shrinking to a Planet, and the indigo firmament sowing itself with daylight stars; easy for you, for me; but whither does it lead? I dread always, to inanity and mere injuring of the lungs!" — with more of the same sort.

On the other hand, Emerson evidently tires of Carlyle's long-winded heroes. He would have him give us the gist of the matter in a few sentences. Cremate your heroes, he seems to say; get all this

gas and water out of them, and give us the handful
of lime and iron of which they are composed. He
hungered for the "central monosyllables." He
praises Cromwell and Frederick, yet says to his
friend, "that book will not come which I most
wish to read, namely, the culled results, the quintessence of private conviction, a *liber veritatis*, a
few sentences, hints of the final moral you drew
from so much penetrating inquest into past and
present men."

This is highly characteristic of Emerson; his bid
for the quintessence of things. He was always
impatient of creative imaginative works; would sub-
lunate or evaporate them in a hurry. Give him
the pith of the matter, the net result in the most
pungent words. It must still be picture and para-
ble, but in a sort of disembodied or potential state.
He fed on the marrow of Shakespeare's sentences,
and apparently cared little for his marvelous characterizations. One is reminded of the child's riddle:
Under the hill there is a mill, in the mill there is
a chest, in the chest there is a till, in the till there
is a phial, in the phial there is a drop I would not
give for all the world. This drop Emerson would
have. Keep or omit the chest and the mill and
all that circumlocution, and give him the precious
essence. But the artistic or creative mind does not
want things thus abridged, — does not want the
universe reduced to an epigram. Carlyle wants an
actual flesh-and-blood hero, and, what is more, wants
him immersed head and ears in the actual affairs of
this world.

Those who seek to explain Carlyle on the ground of his humble origin shoot wide of the mark. "Merely a peasant with a glorified intellect," says a certain irate female masquerading as the "Day of Judgment."

It seems to me Carlyle was as little of a peasant as any man of his time, — a man without one peasant trait or proclivity, a regal and dominating man, "looking," as he said of one of his own books, "king and beggar in the face with an indifference of brotherhood and an indifference of contempt." The two marks of the peasant are stolidity and abjectness; he is dull and heavy, and he dare not say his soul is his own. No man ever so hustled and jostled titled dignitaries, and made them toe the mark, as did Carlyle. It was not merely that his intellect was towering; it was also his character, his will, his standard of manhood, that was towering. He bowed to the hero, to valor and personal worth, never to titles or conventions. The virtues and qualities of his yeoman ancestry were in him without doubt; his power of application, the spirit of toil that possessed him, his frugal, self-denying habits, came from his family and race, but these are not peasant traits, but heroic traits. A certain coarseness of fibre he had also, together with great delicacy and sensibility, but these again he shares with all strong first-class men. You cannot get such histories as Cromwell and Frederick out of polished *littérateurs ;* you must have a man of the same heroic fibre, of the same inexpugnableness of

mind and purpose. Not even was Emerson ade
quate to such a task; he was fine enough and high
enough, but he was not coarse enough and broad
enough. The scholarly part of Carlyle's work is
nearly always thrown in the shade by the manly
part, the original raciness and personal intensity of
the writer. He is not in the least veiled or hidden
by his literary vestments. He is rather hampered
by them, and his sturdy Annandale character often
breaks through them in the most surprising manner.
His contemporaries soon discovered that if here was
a great writer, here was also a great man, come not
merely to paint their picture. but to judge them, to
weigh them in the balance. He is eminently an
artist, and yet it is not the artistic or literary
impulse that lies at the bottom of his works, but
a moral, human, emotional impulse and attraction,
— the impulse of justice, of veracity, or of sympathy and love.

What love of work well done, what love of genuine leadership, of devotion to duty, of mastery of
affairs, in fact what love of man pure and simple,
lies at the bottom of "Frederick," lies at the bottom of "Cromwell"! Here is not the disinterestedness of Shakespeare, here is not the Hellenic
flexibility of mind and scientific impartiality Mr.
Arnold demands: here is espousal, here is vindica-
tion, here is the moral bias of the nineteenth century. But here also is *reality*, here is the creative
touch, here are men and things made alive again,
palpable to the understanding and enticing to the

imagination. Of all histories that have fallen into my hands, "Frederick" is the most vital and real. If the current novels were half so entertaining, I fear I should read little else. The portrait-painting is like that of Rembrandt; the eye for battles and battle-fields is like that of Napoleon, or Frederick himself; the sifting of events, and the separating of the false from the true, is that of the most patient and laborious science; the descriptive passages are equaled by those of no other man; while the work as a whole, as Emerson says, "is a Judgment Day, for its moral verdict, on the men and nations and manners of modern times." It is to be read for its honest history; it is to be read for its inexhaustible wit and humor; it is to be read for its poetic fire, for its felicities of style, for its burden of human sympathy and effort, its heroic attractions and stimulating moral judgments. All Carlyle's histories have the quick, penetrating glance, that stroke of the eye, as the French say, that lays the matter open to the heart. He did not write in the old way of a topographical survey of the surface: his "French Revolution" is more like a transverse section; more like a geologist's map than like a geographer's; the depths are laid open; the abyss yawns; the cosmic forces and fires stalk forth and become visible and real. It was this power to detach and dislocate things and project them against the light of a fierce and lurid imagination that makes his pages unique and matchless, of their kind, in literature. He may be deficient in the historical sense, the sense of development, and of compensation in history; but in vividness of apprehension of men and events, and power of portraiture, he is undoubtedly without a rival. "Those devouring eyes and that portraying hand," Emerson says.

Those who contract their view of Carlyle till they see only his faults do a very unwise thing. Nearly all his great traits have their shadows. His power of characterization sometimes breaks away into caricature; his command of the picturesque leads him into the grotesque; his eloquent denunciation at times becomes vituperation; his marvelous power to name things degenerates into outrageous nicknaming; his streaming humor, which, as Emerson said, floats every object he looks upon, is not free from streaks of the most crabbed, hide-bound ill-humor. Nearly every page has a fringe of these things, and sometimes a pretty broad one, but they are by no means the main matter, and often lend an additional interest. The great personages, the great events, are never caricatured, though painted with a bold, free hand, but there is in the border of the picture all manner of impish and grotesque strokes. In "Frederick" there is a whole series of secondary men and incidents that are touched off with the hand of a master caricaturist. Some peculiarity of feature or manner is seized upon, magnified, and made prominent on all occasions. We are never suffered to forget George the Second's fish eyes and gartered leg; nor the lean May-pole mistress of George the First;

nor the Czarina's big fat cheek; nor poor Bruhl, "vainest of human clothes-horses," with his twelve tailors and his three hundred and sixty-five suits of clothes; nor Augustus, "the dilapidated strong," with his three hundred and fifty-four bastards. Nor can any reader of that work ever forget "Jenkins' Ear," — the poor fraction of an ear of an English sailor snipped off by the Spaniards, and here made to stand for a whole series of historical events. Indeed, this severed ear looms up till it becomes like a sign in the zodiac of those times. His portrait of the French army, which he calls the Dauphiness, is unforgetable, and is in the best style of his historical caricature. It makes its exit over the Rhine before Duke Ferdinand, "much in rags, much in disorder, in terror, and here and there almost in despair, winging their way like clouds of draggled poultry caught by a mastiff in the corn. Across Weser, across Ems, finally across the Rhine itself, every feather of them, — their long-drawn cackle, of a shrieky type, filling all nature in those months." A good sample of the grotesque in Carlyle, pushed to the last limit, and perhaps a little beyond, is in this picture of the Czarina of Russia, stirred up to declare war against Frederick by his Austrian enemies: "Bombarded with cunningly-devised fabrications, every wind freighted for her with phantasmal rumors, no ray of direct daylight visiting the poor Sovereign Woman; who is lazy, not malignant, if she could avoid it; mainly a mass of esurient oil, with alkali on the back of alkali poured in, at this rate for ten years past, till, by pouring and by stirring, they get her to the state of *soap* and froth."

Carlyle had a narrow escape from being the most formidable blackguard the world had ever seen; was, indeed, in certain moods, a kind of divine blackguard, — a purged and pious Rabelais, who could bespatter the devil with more telling epithets than any other man who ever lived. What a tongue, what a vocabulary! He fairly oxidizes, burns up, the object of his opprobrium, in the stream of caustic epithets he turns upon it. He had a low opinion of the contemporaries of Frederick and Voltaire: they were "mere ephemera; contemporary eaters, scramblers for provender, talkers of acceptable hearsay; and related merely to the butteries and wiggeries of their time, and not related to the Perennialities at all, as these two were." He did not have to go very far from home for some of the lineaments of Voltaire's portrait: "He had, if no big gloomy devil in him among the bright angels that were there, a multitude of ravening, tumultuary imps, or little devils, very *ill-chained*, and was lodged, he and his restless little devils, in a skin far too thin for him and them!"

Of Frederick's cynicism he says there was "always a kind of vinegar cleanness in it, *except* in theory." Equally original and felicitous is the "albuminous simplicity" which he ascribes to the Welfs. Newspaper men have never forgiven him for calling them the "gazetteer owls of Minerva;"

and our Catholic brethren can hardly relish his reference to the "consolations" the nuns deal out to the sick as "poisoned gingerbread." In "Frederick" one comes upon such phrases as "milk-faced," "bead-roll histories," "heavy pipe-clay natures," a "stiff-jointed, algebraic kind of piety," etc.

Those who persist in trying Carlyle as a philosopher and man of ideas miss his purport. He had no philosophy, and laid claim to none, except what he got from the German metaphysicians, — views which crop out here and there in "Sartor." He was a preacher of righteousness to his generation, and a rebuker of its shams and irreverences, and as such he cut deep, cut to the bone, and to the marrow of the bone. That piercing, agonized, prophetic, yet withal melodious and winsome voice, how it rises through and above the multitudinous hum and clatter of contemporary voices in England, and alone falls upon the ear as from out the primal depths of moral conviction and power! He is the last man in the world to be reduced to a system or tried by logical tests. You might as well try to bind the sea with chains. His appeal is to the intuitions, the imagination, the moral sense. His power of mental abstraction was not great; he could not deal in abstract ideas. When he attempted to state his philosophy, as in the fragment called "Spiritual Optics," which Froude gives, he is far from satisfactory. His mathematical proficiency seemed to avail him but little in the region of pure ideality. His mind is precipitated at once upon

the concrete, upon actual persons and events. This
makes him the artist he is, as distinguished from
the mystic and philosopher, and is perhaps the basis
of Emerson's remark, that there is "more character
than intellect in every sentence;" that is, more
motive, more will power, more stress of conscience,
more that appeals to one as a living personal iden-
tity, wrestling with facts and events, than there is
that appeals to him as a contemplative philosopher.

Carlyle owed everything to his power of will and
to his unflinching adherence to principle. He was
in no sense a lucky man, had no good fortune, was
borne by no current, was favored ar.d helped by no
circumstance whatever. His life from the first was
a steady pull against both wind and tide. He confronted all the cherished thoughts, beliefs, tendencies, of his time; he spurned and insulted his age
and country. No man ever before poured out such
withering scorn upon his contemporaries. Many of
his political tracts are as blasting as the Satires of
Juvenal. The opinions and practices of his times,
in politics, religion, and literature, were as a stubbly,
brambly field, to which he would fain apply the
match and clean the ground for a nobler crop. He
would purge and fertilize the soil by fire. His
attitude was one of warning and rebuking. He was
refused every public place he ever aspired to, —
every college and editorial chair. Every man's
hand was against him. He was hated by the
Whigs and feared by the Tories. He was poor,
proud, uncompromising, sarcastic; he was morose,

dyspeptic, despondent, compassed about by dragons
and all manner of evil menacing forms; in fact, the
odds were fearfully against him, and yet he succeeded, and succeeded on his own terms. He fairly
conquered the world; yes, and the flesh and the
devil. But it was one incessant, heroic struggle
and wrestle from the first. All through his youth
and his early manhood he was nerving himself for
the conflict. Whenever he took counsel with himself it was to give his courage a new fillip. In his
letters to his people, in his private journal, in all his
meditations, he never loses the opportunity to take
a new hitch upon his resolution, to screw his purpose up tighter. Not a moment's relaxation, but
ceaseless vigilance and "desperate hope." In 1830
he says in his journal: "Oh, I care not for poverty,
little even for disgrace, nothing at all for want of
renown. But the horrible feeling is when I cease
my own struggle, lose the consciousness of my own
strength, and become positively quite worldly and
wicked." A year later he wrote: "To it, thou
Taugenichts! Gird thyself! stir! struggle! forward! forward! Thou art bundled up here and
tied as in a sack. On, then, as in a sack race;
running, not raging!" Carlyle made no terms with
himself nor with others. He would not agree to
keep the peace; he would be the voice of absolute
conscience, of absolute justice, come what come
might. "Woe to them that are at ease in Zion,"
he once said to John Sterling. The stern, uncompromising front which he first turned to the world

he never relaxed for a moment. He had his way
with mankind at all times; or rather conscience
had its way with him at all times in his relations
with mankind. He made no selfish demands, but
ideal demands. Jeffries, seeing his attitude and
his earnestness in it, despaired of him; he looked
upon him as a man butting his head against a stone
wall; he never dreamed that the wall would give
way before the head did. It was not mere obsti-
nacy; it was not the pride of opinion: it was the
thunders of conscience, the awful voice of Sinai,
within him; he *dared* not do otherwise.

A selfish or self-seeking man Carlyle in no sense
was, though it has so often been charged upon him.
He was the victim of his own genius; and he made
others its victims, not of his selfishness. This
genius, no doubt, came nearer the demon of Socrates
than that of any modern man. He is under its
lash and tyranny from first to last. But the watchword of his life was "*Entsagen,*" renunciation, self-
denial, which he learned from Goethe. His demon
did not possess him lightly, but dominated and
drove him.

One would as soon accuse St. Simeon Stylites,
thirty years at the top of his penitential pillar, of
selfishness. Seeking his own ends, following his
own demon, St. Simeon certainly was; but seeking
his ease or pleasure, or animated by any unworthy,
ignoble purpose, he certainly was not. No more
was Carlyle, each one of whose books was a sort of
pillar of penitence or martydom atop of which he

wrought and suffered, shut away from the world, renouncing its pleasures and prizes, wrapped in deepest gloom and misery, and wrestling with all manner of real and imaginary demons and hindrances. During his last great work, — the thirteen years spent in his study at the top of his house, writing the history of Frederick, — this isolation, this incessant toil and penitential gloom, were such as only religious devotees have voluntarily imposed upon themselves.

If Carlyle was "ill to live with," as his mother said, it was not because he was selfish. He was a man, to borrow one of Emerson's early phrases, "inflamed to a fury of personality." He must of necessity assert himself; he is shot with great velocity; he is keyed to an extraordinary pitch; and it was this, this raging fever of individuality, if any namable trait or quality, rather than anything lower in the scale, that often made him an uncomfortable companion and neighbor.

And it may be said here that his wife had the same complaint, and had it bad, the feminine form of it, and without the vent and assuagement of it that her husband found in literature. Little wonder that between two such persons, living childless together for forty years, each assiduously cultivating their sensibilities and idiosyncrasies, there should have been more or less frictions. Both sarcastic, quick-witted, plain-spoken, sleepless, addicted to morphia and blue-pills, nerves all on the outside; the wife without any occupation adequate

to her genius, the husband toiling like Hercules at
his tasks and groaning much louder; both flouting
at happiness; both magnifying the petty ills of life
into harrowing tragedies; both gifted with "preter-
natural intensity of sensation;" Mrs. C. nearly
killed by the sting of a wasp; Mr. C. driven nearly
distracted by the crowing of a cock or the baying
of a dog; the wife hot-tempered, the husband atra-
bilarious; one caustic, the other arrogant; marrying
from admiration rather than from love — could one
reasonably predict, beforehand, a very high state
of domestic felicity for such a couple? and would
it be just to lay the blame all on the husband, as
has generally been done in this case? Man and
wife were too much alike; the marriage was in no
sense a union of opposites; at no point did the two
sufficiently offset and complement each other; hence,
though deeply devoted, they never seemed to find
the repose and the soothing acquiescence in the
society of one another that marriage should bring.
They both had the great virtues, — nobleness, gen-
erosity, courage, deep kindliness, etc., — but neither of them had the small virtues. Both gave
way under small annoyances, paltry cares, petty
interruptions, — bugs, cocks, donkeys, street noises,
etc. To great emergencies, to great occasions, they
could oppose great qualities; there can be no doubt
of that, but the ordinary every-day hindrances and
petty burdens of life fretted their spirits into tatters. Mrs. C. used frequently to return from her
trips to the country with her "mind all churned

into froth," — no butter of sweet thought or sweet content at all. Yet Carlyle could say of her, "Not a bad little dame at all. She and I did aye very weel together; and 'tweel, it was not every one that could have done with her," which was doubtless the exact truth. Froude also speaks from personal knowledge when he says: "His was the soft heart and hers the stern one."

We are now close on to the cardinal fact of Carlyle's life and teachings, namely, the urgency of his quest for heroes and heroic qualities. This is the master key to him; the main stress of his preaching and writing is here. He is the medium and exemplar of the value of personal force and prowess, and he projected this thought into current literature and politics, with the emphasis of gunpowder and torpedoes. He had a vehement and overweening conceit in man. A sort of anthropomorphic greed and hunger possessed him always, an insatiable craving for strong, picturesque characters, and for contact and conflict with them. This was his ruling passion (and it amounted to a passion) all his days. He fed his soul on heroes and heroic qualities, and all his literary exploits were a search for these things. Where he found them not, where he did not come upon some trace of them in books, in society, in politics, he saw only barrenness and futility. He was an idealist who was inhospitable to ideas; he must have a man, the flavor and stimulus of ample concrete personalities. "In the country," he said, writing to his brother in 1821, "I am like an alien, a stranger and pilgrim from a far-distant land." His faculties were "up in mutiny, and slaying one another for lack of fair enemies." He must to the city, to Edinburgh, and finally to London, where, thirteen years later, we find his craving as acute as ever. "Oct. 1st. This morning think of the old primitive Edinburgh scheme of *engineership;* almost meditate for a moment resuming it *yet!* It were a method of gaining bread, of getting into contact with men, my two grand wants and prayers."

Nothing but man, but heroes, touched him, moved him, satisfied him. He stands for heroes and hero-worship, and for that alone. Bring him the most plausible theory, the most magnanimous idea in the world, and he is cold, indifferent, or openly insulting; but bring him a brave, strong man, or the reminiscence of any noble personal trait, — sacrifice, obedience, reverence, — and every faculty within him stirs and responds. Dreamers and enthusiasts, with their schemes for the millennium, rushed to him for aid and comfort, and usually had the door slammed in their faces. They forgot it was a man he had advertised for, and not an idea. Indeed, if you had the blow-fly of any popular ism or reform buzzing in your bonnet, No. 5 Cheyne Row was the house above all others to be avoided; little chance of inoculating such a mind as Carlyle's with your notions, — of *blowing* a toiling and sweating hero at his work. But welcome to any man with real work to do and the

courage to do it; welcome to any man who stood
for any real, tangible thing in his own right.   "In
God's name, what *art* thou?   Not Nothing, sayest
thou!   Then, How much and what?   This is the
thing I would know, and even *must* soon know,
such a pass am I come to!"   ("Past and Present.")

Caroline Fox, in her Memoirs, tells how, in
1842, Carlyle's sympathies were enlisted in behalf
of a Cornish miner who had kept his place in the
bottom of a shaft, above a blast the fuse of which
had been prematurely lighted, and allowed his com-
rades to be hauled up when only one could escape
at a time.   He inquired out the hero, who, as by
miracle, had survived the explosion, and set on
foot an enterprise to raise funds for the bettering
of his condition.   In a letter to Sterling, he said
there was help and profit in knowing that there
was such a true and brave workman living, and
working with him on the earth at that time.   "Tell
all the people," he said, "that a man of this kind
ought to be hatched, — that it were shameful to eat
him as a breakfast egg!"

All Carlyle's sins of omission and commission
grew out of this terrible predilection for the individual hero: this bent or inclination determined the
whole water-shed, so to speak, of his mind; every
rill and torrent swept swiftly and noisily in this
one direction.   It is the tragedy in Burns's life that
attracts him; the morose heroism in Johnson's, the
copious manliness in Scott's, the lordly and regal
quality in Goethe.   Emerson praised Plato to him;

but the endless dialectical hair-splitting of the Greek philosopher, — "how does all this concern me at all?" he said. But when he discovered that Plato hated the Athenian democracy most cordially, and poured out his scorn upon it, he thought much better of him. History swiftly resolves itself into biography to him; the tide in the affairs of men ebbed and flowed in obedience to the few potent wills. We do not find him exploiting or elucidating ideas and principles, but moral qualities, — always on the scent, on the search of the heroic.

He raises aloft the standard of the individual will, the supremacy of man over events. He sees the reign of law; none see it clearer. "Eternal Law is silently present everywhere and everywhen. By Law the Planets gyrate in their orbits; by some approach to Law the street-cabs ply in their thoroughfares." But law is still personal will with him, the will of God. He can see nothing but individuality, but conscious will and force, in the universe. He believed in a personal God. He had an inward ground of assurance of it in his own intense personality and vivid apprehension of personal force and genius. He seems to have believed in a personal devil. At least he abuses "Auld Nickie-Ben" as one would hardly think of abusing an abstraction. However impractical we may regard Carlyle, he was entirely occupied with practical questions; an idealist turned loose, in the actual affairs of this world, and intent only on bettering them. That which so drew reformers and all ardent

ideal natures to him was not the character of his
conviction, but the torrid impetuosity of his belief.
He had the earnestness of fanaticism, the earnestness of rebellion; the earnestness of the Long Parliament and the National Convention, — the only
two parliaments he praises.   He did not merely see
the truth and placidly state it, standing aloof and
apart from it; but, as soon as his intellect had con-
ceived a thing as true, every current of his being
set swiftly in that direction; it was an outlet at
once for his whole pent-up energies, and there was
a flood and sometimes an inundation of Carlylean
wrath and power.   Coming from Goethe, with his
marvelous insight and cool, uncommitted moral
nature, to the great Scotchman, is like coming from
dress parade to a battle, from Melancthon to Luther.
It would be far from the truth to say that Goethe
was not in earnest: he was all eyes, all vision; he
saw everything, but saw it for his own ends and
behoof, for contemplation and enjoyment.   In Carlyle the vision is productive of pain and suffering,
because his moral nature sympathizes so instantly
and thoroughly with his intellectual; it is a call
to battle, and every faculty is enlisted.   It was
this that made Carlyle akin to the reformers and
the fanatics, and led them to expect more of him
than they got.   The artist element in him, and his
vital hold upon the central truths of character and
personal force, saved him from any such fate as
overtook his friend Irving.

Out of Carlyle's fierce and rampant individualism

come his grasp of character and his power of human portraiture. It is, perhaps, not too much to say, that in all literature there is not another such a master portrait-painter, such a limner and interpreter of historical figures and physiognomies. That power of the old artists to paint or to carve a man, to body him forth, almost re-create him, so rare in the moderns, Carlyle had in a preëminent degree. As an artist it is his distinguishing gift, and puts him on a par with Rembrandt, Angelo, Reynolds, and with the antique masters of sculpture. He could put his finger upon the weak point and upon the strong point of a man as unerringly as fate. He knew a man as a jockey knows a horse. His pictures of Johnson, of Boswell, of Voltaire, of Mirabeau, what masterpieces! His portrait of Coleridge will doubtless survive all others, inadequate as it is in many ways; one fears, also that poor Lamb has been stamped to last. None of Carlyle's characterizations have excited more ill-feeling than this same one of Lamb. But it was plain from the outset that Carlyle could not like such a verbal acrobat as Lamb. He doubtless had him or his kind in view when he wrote this passage in "Past and Present:" "His poor fraction of sense has to be perked into some epigrammatic shape, that it may prick into me, — perhaps (this is the commonest) to be topsy-turvied, left standing on its head, that I may remember it the better! Such grinning insanity is very sad to the soul of man. Human faces should not grin on one like masks; they

should look on one like faces! I love honest laugh-
ter as I do sunlight, but not dishonest; most kinds
of dancing, too, but the St. Vitus kind, not at
all!"

If Carlyle had taken to the brush instead of to
the pen, he would probably have left a gallery of
portraits such as this century has not seen. In his
letters, journals, reminiscences, etc., for him to
mention a man is to describe his face, and with
what graphic pen-and-ink sketches they abound!
Let me extract a few of them. Here is Rousseau's
face, from "Heroes and Hero Worship:" "A high
but narrow-contracted intensity in it; bony brows;
deep, straight-set eyes, in which there is something
bewildered - looking, — bewildered, peering with
lynx-eagerness; a face full of misery, even ignoble
misery, and also of an antagonism against that;
something mean, plebeian, there, redeemed only by
intensity ; the face of what is called a fanatic, —
a sadly *contracted* hero!" Here a glimpse of Dan-
ton: "Through whose black brows and rude, flat-
tened face there looks a waste energy as of Hercules." Camille Desmoulins: "With the face of
dingy blackguardism, wondrously irradiated with
genius, as if a naphtha lamp burned in it." Through
Mirabeau's "shaggy, beetle-brows, and rough-hewn,
seamed, carbuncled face there look natural ugliness,
smallpox, incontinence, bankruptcy, and burning
fire of genius; like comet fire, glaring fuliginous
through murkiest confusions."

On first meeting with John Stuart Mill he de-

scribes him to his wife as "a slender, rather tall,
and elegant youth, with small, clear, Roman-nosed
face, two small, earnestly smiling eyes; modest,
remarkably gifted with precision of utterance; en-
thusiastic, yet lucid, calm; not a great, yet distinctly a gifted and amiable youth."

A London editor, whom he met about the same
time, he describes as "a tall, loose, lank-haired,
wrinkly, wintry, vehement-looking flail of a man."
He goes into the House of Commons on one of his
early visits to London: "Althorp spoke, a thick,
large, broad-whiskered, farmer-looking man; Hume
also, a powdered, clean, burly fellow; and Weth-
erell, a beetle-browed, sagacious, quizzical old gentleman; then Davies, a Roman-nosed dandy," etc.
He must touch off the portrait of every man he
sees.   De Quincey "is one of the smallest men you
ever in your life beheld; but with a most gentle
and sensible face, only that the teeth are destroyed
by opium, and the little bit of an under lip projects
like a shelf."   Leigh Hunt: "Dark complexion (a
trace of the African, I believe); copious, clean,
strong black hair, beautifully shaped head, fine,
beaming, serious hazel eyes; seriousness and intellect the main expression of the face (to our surprise
at first)."

Here is his sketch of Tennyson: "A fine, large-
featured, dim-eyed, bronze-colored, shaggy-headed
man is Alfred; dusty, smoky, free and easy, who
swings outwardly and inwardly with great composure in an inarticulate element of tranquil chaos and

tobacco smoke. Great now and then when he does emerge, — a most restful, brotherly, solid-hearted man."

Here we have Dickens in 1840: "Clear blue intelligent eyes; eyebrows that he arches amazingly; large, protrusive, rather loose mouth; a face of most extreme *mobility*, which he shuttles about — eyebrows, eyes, mouth, and all — in a very singular manner while speaking. Surmount this with a loose coil of common-colored hair, and set it on a small compact figure, very small, and dressed à la D'Orsay rather than well, — this is Pickwick."

Here is a glimpse of Grote, the historian of Greece: "A man with straight upper lip, large chin, and open mouth (spout mouth); for the rest, a tall man, with dull, thoughtful brow and lank, disheveled hair, greatly the look of a prosperous Dissenting minister."

In telling Emerson whom he shall see in London, he says: "Southey's complexion is still healthy mahogany brown, with a fleece of white hair, and eyes that seem running at full gallop; old Rogers, with his pale head, white, bare, and cold as snow, with those large blue eyes, cruel, sorrowful, and that sardonic shelf chin."

In another letter he draws this portrait of Webster: "As a logic-fencer, advocate, or parliamentary Hercules, one would incline to back him, at first sight, against all the extant world. The tanned complexion; that amorphous crag-like face; the dull black eyes under their precipice of brows like dull anthracite furnaces, needing only to be *blown;* the mastiff-mouth accurately closed: I have not traced as much of *silent Berserker rage*, that I remember of, in any other man." In writing his histories Carlyle valued, above almost anything else, a good portrait of his hero, and searched far and wide for such. He roamed through endless picture-galleries in Germany searching for a genuine portrait of Frederick the Great, and at last, chiefly by good luck, hit upon the thing he was in quest of. "If one would buy an indisputably authentic *old shoe* of William Wallace for hundreds of pounds, and run to look at it from all ends of Scotland, what would one give for an authentic visible shadow of his face, could such, by art natural or art magic, now be had!" "Often I have found a Portrait superior in real instruction to half a dozen written 'Biographies,' as Biographies are written; or, rather, let me say, I have found that the Portrait was a small lighted *candle* by which the Biographies could for the first time be *read*, and some human interpretation be made of them."

II

Carlyle stands at all times, at all places, for the hero, for power of will, authority of character, adequacy, and obligation of personal force. He offsets completely, and with the emphasis of a clap of thunder, the modern leveling impersonal tendencies, the "manifest destinies," the blind mass movements, the merging of the one in the many, the rule of majorities, the no-government, no-leadership, *laissez-faire* principle. Unless there was evidence of a potent, supreme, human will guiding affairs, he had no faith in the issue; unless the hero was in the saddle, and the dumb blind forces well bitted and curbed beneath him, he took no interest in the venture. The cause of the North, in the War of the Rebellion, failed to enlist him or touch him. It was a people's war; the hand of the strong man was not conspicuous; it was a conflict of ideas, rather than of personalities; there was no central and dominating figure around which events revolved. He missed his Cromwell, his Frederick. So far as his interest was aroused at all, it was with the South, because he had heard of the Southern slave-driver; he knew Cuffee had a master, and the crack of his whip was sweeter music to him than the crack of antislavery rifles, behind which he recognized only a vague, misdirected philanthropy.

Carlyle did not see things in their relation, or as a philosopher; he saw them detached, and hence more or less in conflict and opposition. We accuse him of wrong-headedness, but it is rather inflexibleness of mind and temper. He is not a brook that flows, but a torrent that plunges and plows. He tried poetry, he tried novel-writing in his younger days, but he had not the flexibility of spirit to succeed in these things; his moral vehemence, his fury of conviction, were too great.

Great is the power of reaction in the human

body; great is the power of reaction and recoil in all organic nature. But apparently there was no power of reaction in Carlyle's mind; he never reacts from his own extreme views; never looks for the compensations, never seeks to place himself at the point of equilibrium, or adjusts his view to other related facts. He saw the value of the hero, the able man, and he precipitated himself upon this fact with such violence, so detached it and magnified it, that it fits with no modern system of things. He was apparently entirely honest in his conviction that modern governments and social organizations were rushing swiftly to chaos and ruin, because the hero, the natural leader, was not at the head of affairs, — overlooking entirely the many checks and compensations, and ignoring the fact that, under a popular government especially, nations are neither made nor unmade by the wisdom or folly of their rulers, but by the character for wisdom and virtue of the mass of their citizens. "Where the great mass of men is tolerably right," he himself says, "all is right; where they are not right, all is wrong." What difference can it make to America, for instance, to the real growth and prosperity of the nation, whether the ablest man goes to Congress or fills the Presidency or the second or third ablest? The most that we can expect, in ordinary times at least, is that the machinery of universal suffrage will yield us a fair sample of the leading public man, — a man who fairly represents the average ability and average honesty of the better class of the citizens. In extraordinary times, in times of national peril, when there is a real strain upon the state, and the instinct of self-preservation comes into play, then fate itself brings forward the ablest men. The great crisis makes or discovers the great man, — discovers Cromwell, Frederick, Washington, Lincoln. Carlyle leaves out of his count entirely the competitive principle that operates everywhere in nature, — in your field and garden as well as in political states and amid teeming populations, — natural selection, the survival of the fittest. Under artificial conditions the operation of this law is more or less checked; but amid the struggles and parturition throes of a people, artificial conditions disappear, and we touch real ground at last. What a sorting and sifting process went on in our army during the secession war, till the real captains, the real leaders, were found; not Fredericks, or Wellingtons, perhaps, but the best the land afforded!

The object of popular government is no more to find and elevate the hero, the man of special and exceptional endowment, into power, than the object of agriculture is to take the prizes at the agricultural fairs. It is one of the things to be hoped for and aspired to, but not one of the indispensables. The success of free government is attained when it has made the people independent of special leaders, and secured the free and full expression of the popular will and conscience. Any view of American politics, based upon the failure of the suffrage always, or even generally, to lift into power the ablest men, is partial and unscientific. We can stand, and have stood, any amount of mediocrity in our appointed rulers; and perhaps in the ordinary course of events mediocrity is the safest and best. We could no longer surrender ourselves to great leaders, if we wanted to. Indeed, there is no longer a call for great leaders; with the appearance of the people upon the scene, the hero must await his orders. How often in this country have the people checked and corrected the folly and wrong-headedness of their rulers! It is probably true, as Carlyle says, that "the smallest item of human Slavery is the oppression of man by his Mock-Superiors;" but shall we accept the other side of the proposition, that the grand problem is to find government by our Real Superiors? The grand problem is rather to be superior to all government, and to possess a nationality that finally rests upon principles quite beyond the fluctuations of ordinary politics. A people possessed of the gift of Empire, like the English stock, both in Europe and in America, are in our day beholden very little to their chosen rulers. Otherwise the English nation would have been extinct long ago.

"Human virtue," Carlyle wrote in 1850, "if we went down to the roots of it, is not so rare. The materials of human virtue are everywhere abundant as the light of the sun." This may well offset his more pessimistic statement, that "there are fools, cowards, knaves, and gluttonous traitors, true only to their own appetite, in immense majority in every rank of life; and there is nothing frightfuller than to see these voting and deciding." If we "went down to the roots of it," this statement is simply untrue. "Democracy," he says, "is, by the nature of it, a self-canceling business, and gives, in the long run, a net result of *zero.*"

Because the law of gravitation is uncompromising, things are not, therefore, crushed in a wild rush to the centre of attraction. The very traits that make Carlyle so entertaining and effective as a historian and biographer, namely, his fierce, man-devouring eyes, make him impracticable in the sphere of practical politics.

Let me quote a long and characteristic passage from Carlyle's Latter-Day Pamphlets, one of dozens of others, illustrating his misconception of universal suffrage: —

"Your ship cannot double Cape Horn by its excellent plans of voting. The ship may vote this and that, above decks and below, in the most harmonious, exquisitely constitutional manner; the ship, to get round Cape Horn, will find a set of conditions already voted for and fixed with adamantine rigor by the ancient Elemental Powers, who are entirely careless how you vote. If you can, by voting or without voting, ascertain these conditions, and valiantly conform to them, you will get around the Cape: if you cannot, the ruffian winds will blow you ever back again; the inexorable Icebergs, dumb privy-councilors from Chaos, will nudge you with most chaotic ' admonition; ' you will be flung

half frozen on the Patagonian cliffs, or admonished
into shivers by your iceberg councilors and sent
sheer down to Davy Jones, and will never get
around Cape Horn at all! Unanimity on board
ship; — yes, indeed, the ship's crew may be very
unanimous, which, doubtless, for the time being,
will be very comfortable to the ship's crew and to
their Phantasm Captain, if they have one; but if
the tack they unanimously steer upon is guiding
them into the belly of the Abyss, it will not profit
them much! Ships, accordingly, do not use the
ballot-box at all; and they reject the Phantasm
species of Captain. One wishes much some other
Entities — since all entities lie under the same rig-
orous set of laws — could be brought to show as
much wisdom and sense at least of self-preservation,
the *first* command of nature. Phantasm Captains
with unanimous votings, — this is considered to be
all the law and all the prophets at present."

This has the real crushing Carlylean wit and picturesqueness of statement, but is it the case of
democracy, of universal suffrage fairly put? The
eternal verities appear again, as they appear everywhere in our author in connection with this subject. They recur in his pages like "minute-guns,"
as if deciding, by the count of heads, whether
Jones or Smith should go to Parliament or to Congress was equivalent to sitting in judgment upon
the law of gravitation. What the ship in doubling
Cape Horn would very likely do, if it found itself
officerless, would be to choose, by some method

more or less approaching a count of heads, a captain, an ablest man to take command, and put the vessel through. If none were able, then indeed the case were desperate; with or without the ballot-box, the abyss would be pretty sure of a victim. In any case there would perhaps be as little voting to annul the storms, or change the ocean currents, as there is in democracies to settle ethical or scientific principles by an appeal to universal suffrage. But Carlyle was fated to see the abyss lurking under, and the eternities presiding over, every act of life. He saw everything in fearful gigantic perspective. It is true that one cannot loosen the latchet of his shoe without bending to forces that are cosmical, sidereal; but whether he bends or not, or this way or that, he passes no verdict upon them. The temporary, the expedient, — all those devices and adjustments that are of the nature of scaffolding, and that enter so largely into the administration of the coarser affairs of this world, — were with Carlyle equivalent to the false, the sham, the phantasmal, and he would none of them. As the ages seem to have settled themselves for the present and the future, in all civilized countries, — and especially in America, —politics is little more than scaffolding; it certainly is not the house we live in, but an appurtenance or necessity of the house. A government, in the long run, can never be better or worse than the people governed. In voting for Jones for constable, am I voting for or against the unalterable laws of the universe, — an act whereir

the consequences of a mistake are so appalling that
voting had better be dispensed with, and the selection of constables be left to the evolutionary principle of the solar system?

Carlyle was not a reconciler. When he saw a
fact, he saw it with such intense and magnifying
eyes, as I have already said, that it became at once
irreconcilable with other facts. He could not and
would not reconcile popular government, the rule of
majorities, with what he knew and what we all
know to be popular follies, or the proneness of the
multitude to run after humbugs. How easy for
fallacies, speciosities, quackeries, etc., to become
current! That a thing is popular makes a wise
man look upon it with suspicion. Are the greatest
or best books the most read books? Have not the
great principles, the great reforms, begun in minorities and fought their way against the masses? Does
not the multitude generally greet its saviors with
"Crucify him, crucify him"? Who have been the
martyrs and the persecuted in all ages? Where
does the broad road lead to, and which is the Narrow Way? "Can it be proved that, since the
beginning of the world, there was ever given a universal vote in favor of the worthiest man or thing?
I have always understood that true worth, in any
department, was difficult to recognize; that the
worthiest, if he appealed to universal suffrage,
would have but a poor chance."

Upon these facts Carlyle planted himself, and
the gulf which he saw open between them and the

beauties of universal suffrage was simply immense. Without disputing the facts here, we may ask if they really bear upon the question of popular government, of a free ballot? If so, then the ground is clean shot away from under it. The world is really governed and led by minorities, and always will be. The many, sooner or later, follow the one. We have all become abolitionists in this country, some of us much to our surprise and bewilderment; we hardly know yet how it happened; but the time was when abolitionists were hunted by the multitude. Marvelous to relate, also, civil service reform has become popular among our politicians. Something has happened; the tide has risen while we slept, or while we mocked and laughed, and away we all go on the current. Yet it is equally true that, under any form of government, nothing short of events themselves, nothing short of that combination of circumstances which we name fate or fortune, can place that exceptional man, the hero, at the head of affairs. If there are no heroes, then woe to the people who have lost the secret of producing great men.

The worthiest man usually has other work to do, and avoids politics. Carlyle himself could not be induced to stand for Parliament. "Who would govern," he says, "that can get along without governing? He that is fittest for it is of all men the unwillingest unless constrained." But constrained he cannot be, yet he is our only hope. What shall we do? A government by the fittest can alone save mankind, yet the fittest is not forthcoming. We do not know him; he does not know himself. The case is desperate. Hence the despair of Carlyle in his view of modern politics.

Who that has read his history of Frederick has not at times felt that he would gladly be the subject of a real king like the great Prussian, a king who was indeed the father of his people; a sovereign man at the head of affairs with the reins of government all in his own hands; an imperial husbandman devoted to improving, extending, and building up his nation as the farmer his farm, and toiling as no husbandman ever toiled; a man to reverence, to love, to fear; who called all the women his daughters, and all the men his sons, and whom to see and to speak with was the event of a lifetime; a shepherd to his people, a lion to his enemies? Such a man gives head and character to a nation; he is the head and the people are the body; currents of influence and of power stream down from such a hero to the life of the humblest peasant; his spirit diffuses itself through the nation. It is the ideal state; it is captivating to the imagination; there is an artistic completeness about it. Probably this is why it so captivated Carlyle, inevitable artist that he was. But how impossible to us! how impossible to any English-speaking people by their own action and choice; not because we are unworthy such a man, but because an entirely new order of things has arrived, and arrived in due course of time, through the political and social evolution of

man. The old world has passed away; the age
of the hero, of the strong leader, is gone. The
people have arrived, and sit in judgment upon all
who would rule or lead them. Science has arrived,
everything is upon trial; private judgment is supreme.   Our only hope in this country, at least in
the sphere of governments, is in the collective wisdom of the people; and, as extremes so often meet,
perhaps this, if thoroughly realized, is as complete
and artistic a plan as the others. The "collective
folly" of the people, Carlyle would say, and perhaps during his whole life he never for a moment
saw it otherwise; never saw that the wisdom of
the majority could be other than the no-wisdom
of blind masses of unguided men. He seemed to
forget, or else not to know, that universal suffrage,
as exemplified in America, was really a sorting and
sifting process, a search for the wise, the truly representative man; that the vast masses were not
asked who should rule over them, but were asked
which of two candidates they preferred, in selecting
which candidates what of wisdom and leadership
there was available had had their due weight; in
short, that democracy alone makes way for and offers
a clear road to natural leadership. Under the pressure of opposing parties, all the political wisdom and
integrity there is in the country stand between the
people, the masses, and the men of their choice.

Undoubtedly popular government will, in the
main, be like any other popular thing, — it will
partake of the conditions of popularity; it will

seldom elevate the greatest; it will never elevate
the meanest; it is based upon the average virtue
and intelligence of the people.

There have been great men in all countries and
times who possessed the elements of popularity, and
would have commanded the suffrage of the people;
on the other hand, there have been men who possessed many elements of popularity, but few traits
of true greatness; others with greatness, but no
elements of popularity. These last are the reformers, the innovators, the starters, and their greatness
is a discovery of after-times. Popular suffrage cannot elevate these men, and if, as between the two
other types, it more frequently seizes upon the last,
it is because the former is the more rare.

But there is a good deal of delusion about the
proneness of the multitude to run after quacks and
charlatans: a multitude runs, but a larger multitude
does not run; and those that do run soon see their
mistake. Real worth, real merit, alone wins the
permanent suffrage of mankind. In every neighborhood and community the best men are held in
highest regard by the most persons. The world
over, the names most fondly cherished are those
most worthy of being cherished. Yet this does not
prevent that certain types of great men — men who
are in advance of their times and announce new
doctrines and faiths — will be rejected and denied
by their contemporaries. This is the order of nature.
Minorities lead and save the world, and the world
knows them not till long afterward.

No man perhaps suspects how large and important the region of unconsciousness in him, what a vast, unknown territory lies there back of his conscious will and purpose, and which is really the controlling power of his life. Out of it things arise, and shape and define themselves to his consciousness and rule his career. Here the influence of environment works; here the elements of race, of family; here the Time-Spirit moulds him and he knows it not; here Nature, or Fate, as we sometimes name it, rules him and makes him what he is.

In every people or nation stretches this deep, unsuspected background. Here the great movements begin; here the deep processes go on; here the destiny of the race or nation really lies. In this soil the new ideas are sown; the new man, the despised leader, plants his seed here, and if they be vital they thrive, and in due time emerge and become the conscious possession of the community.

None knew better than Carlyle himself that, whoever be the ostensible potentates and lawmakers, the wise do virtually rule, the natural leaders do lead. Wisdom will out: it is the one thing in this world that cannot be suppressed or annulled. There is not a parish, township, or community, little or big, in this country or in England, that is not finally governed, shaped, directed, built up by what of wisdom there is in it. All the leading industries and enterprises gravitate naturally to the hands best able to control them. The wise

furnish employment for the unwise, capital flows
to capital hands as surely as water seeks water.

> "Winds blow and waters roll
> Strength to the brave."

There never is and never can be any government
but by the wisest. In all nations and communities
the law of nature finally prevails. If there is no
wisdom in the people, there will be none in their
rulers; the virtue and intelligence of the representative will not be essentially different from that of
his constituents. The dependence of the foolish,
the thriftless, the improvident, upon his natural
master and director, for food, employment, for life
itself, is just as real to-day in America as it was in
the old feudal or patriarchal times. The relation
between the two is not so obvious, so intimate, so
voluntary, but it is just as vital and essential. How
shall we know the wise man unless he makes himself felt, or seen, or heard? How shall we know
the master unless he masters us? Is there any
danger that the real captains will not step to the
front, and that we shall not know them when they
do? Shall we not know a Luther, a Cromwell, a
Franklin, a Washington?

"Man," says Carlyle, "little as he may suppose
it, is necessitated to obey superiors; he is a social
being in virtue of this necessity; nay, he could
not be gregarious otherwise; he obeys those whom
he esteems better than himself, wiser, braver, and
will forever obey such; and ever be ready and
delighted to do it." Think in how many ways,

through how many avenues, in our times, the wise man can reach us and place himself at our head, or mould us to his liking, as orator, statesman, poet, philosopher, preacher, editor. If he has any wise mind to speak, any scheme to unfold, there is the rostrum or pulpit and crowds ready to hear him, or there is the steam power press ready to disseminate his wisdom to the four corners of the earth. He can set up a congress or a parliament and really make and unmake the laws, by his own fireside, in any country that has a free press. "If we will consider it, the essential truth of the matter is, every British man can now elect *himself* to Parliament without consulting the hustings at all. If there be any vote, idea, or notion in him, or any earthly or heavenly thing, cannot he take a pen and therewith autocratically pour forth the same into the ears and hearts of all people, so far as it will go?" ("Past and Present.") Or, there is the pulpit everywhere waiting to be worthily filled. What may not the real hero accomplish here? "Indeed, is not this that we call spiritual guidance properly he soul of the whole, the life and eyesight of the whole?" Some one has even said, "Let me make the songs of a nation and I care not who makes the laws." Certainly the great poet of a people is its real Founder and King. He rules for centuries and rules in the heart.

In more primitive times, and amid more rudely organized communities, the hero, the strong man, could step to the front and seize the leadership like

the buffalo of the plains or the wild horse of the
pampas; but in our time, at least among English-
speaking races, he must be more or less called by
the suffrage of the people.   It is quite certain that,
had there been a seventeenth or eighteenth century
Carlyle he would not have seen the hero in Cromwell, or in Frederick, that the nineteenth century
Carlyle saw in each.   In any case, in any event,
the dead rule us more than the living; we cannot
escape the past.   It is not merely by virtue of the
sunlight that falls now, and the rain and dew that
it brings, that we continue here; but by virtue of
the sunlight of æons of past ages.

"This land of England has its conquerors, pos-
sessors, which change from epoch to epoch, from
day to day; but its real conquerors, creators, and
eternal proprietors are these following and their
representatives, if you can find them: all the Heroic
Souls that ever were in England, each in their
degree; all the men that ever cut a thistle, drained
a puddle out of England, contrived a wise scheme
in England, did or said a true and valiant thing in
England."   "Work?   The quantity of done and
forgotten work that lies silent under my feet in this
world, and escorts and attends me and supports and
keeps me alive, wheresoever I walk or stand, what-
soever I think or do, gives rise to reflections!"   In
our own politics, has our first President ever ceased
to be President?   Does he not still sit there, the
stern and blameless patriot, uttering counsel?

Carlyle had no faith in the inherent tendency of

things to right themselves, to adjust themselves to their own proper standards; the conservative force of Nature, the checks and balances by which her own order and succession is maintained; the Darwinian principle, according to which the organic life of the globe has been evolved, the higher and more complex forms mounting from the lower, the true *palingenesia*, the principle or power, name it Fate, name it Necessity, name it God, or what you will, which finally lifts a people, a race, an age, and even a community above the reach of choice, of accident, of individual will, into the region of general law. So little is life what we make it, after all; so little is the course of history, the destiny of nations, the result of any man's purpose, or direction, or will, so great is Fate, so insignificant is man! The human body is made up of a vast congeries or association of minute cells, each with its own proper work and function, at which it toils incessantly night and day, and thinks of nothing beyond. The shape, the size, the color of the body, its degree of health and strength, etc., — no cell or series of cells decides these points; a law above and beyond the cell determines them. The final destiny and summing up of a nation is, perhaps, as little within the conscious will and purpose of the individual citizens. When you come to large masses, to long periods, the law of nature steps in. The day is hot or the day is cold, the spring is late or the spring is early; but the inclination of the earth's axis makes the winter and

summer sure. The wind blows this way and blows
that, but the great storms gyrate and travel in one
general direction. There is a wind of the globe that
never varies, and there is the breeze of the mountain
that is never two days alike. The local hurricane
moves the waters of the sea to a depth of but a
few feet, but the tidal impulse goes to the bottom.
Men and communities in this world are often in the
position of arctic explorers, who are making great
speed in a given direction while the ice-floe beneath
them is making greater speed in the opposite direction. This kind of progress has often befallen
political and ecclesiastical parties in this country.
Behind mood lies temperament; back of the caprice
of will lies the fate of character; back of both is
the bias of family; back of that, the tyranny of
race; still deeper, the power of climate, of soil, of
geology, the whole physical and moral environment.
Still we are free men only so far as we rise above
these. We cannot abolish fate, but we can in a
measure utilize it. The projectile force of the bul-
let does not annul or suspend gravity; it uses it.
The floating vapor is just as true an illustration of
the law of gravity as the falling avalanche.

Carlyle, I say, had sounded these depths that lie
beyond the region of will and choice, beyond the
sphere of man's moral accountability; but in life,
in action, in conduct, no man shall take shelter
here. One may summon his philosophy when he
is beaten in battle, and not till then. You shall
not shirk the hobbling Times to catch a ride on the

sure-footed Eternities. "The times are bad; very
well, you are there to make them better." "The
public highways ought not to be occupied by people
demonstrating that motion is impossible." ("Chart-
ism.")

III

Caroline Fox, in her "Memoirs of Old Friends,"
reports a smart saying about Carlyle, current in her
time, which has been current in some form or other
ever since; namely, that he had a large capital of
faith uninvested, — carried it about him as ready
money, I suppose, working capital. It is certainly
true that it was not locked up in any of the various
social and religious safe-deposits. He employed a
vast deal of it in his daily work. It took not a
little to set Cromwell up, and Frederick. Indeed,
it is doubtful if among his contemporaries there
was a man with so active a faith, — so little invested
in paper securities. His religion, as a present living reality, went with him into every question.
He did not believe that the Maker of this universe
had retired from business, or that he was merely a
sleeping partner in the concern. "Original sin,"
he says, "and such like are bad enough, I doubt
not; but distilled sin, dark ignorance, stupidity,
dark corn-law, bastile and company, what are they ? "
For creeds, theories, philosophies, plans for reform-
ing the world, etc., he cared nothing, he would
not invest one moment in them; but the hero, the
worker, the doer, justice, veracity, courage, these
drew him, — in these he put his faith.   What to

other people were mere abstractions were urgent,
pressing realities to Carlyle. Every truth or fact
with him has a personal inclination, points to conduct, points to duty. He could not invest himself
in creeds and formulas, but in that which yielded
an instant return in force, justice, character. He
has no philosophical impartiality. He has been
broken up; there have been moral convulsions; the
rock stands on end. Hence the vehement and precipitous character of his speech, — its wonderful
picturesqueness and power. The spirit of gloom
and dejection that possesses him, united to such an
indomitable spirit of work and helpfulness, is very
noteworthy. Such courage, such faith, such un-
shaken adamantine belief in the essential soundness
and healthfulness that lay beneath all this weltering
and chaotic world of folly and evil about him, in
conjunction with such pessimism and despondency,
was never before seen in a man of letters. I am
reminded that in this respect he was more like a
root of the tree of Igdrasil than like a branch; one
of the central and master roots, with all that
implies, toiling and grappling in the gloom, but
full of the spirit of light. How he delves and
searches; how much he made live and bloom again;
how he sifted the soil for the last drop of heroic
blood! The Fates are there, too, with water from
the sacred well. He is quick, sensitive, full of
tenderness and pity; yet he is savage and brutal
when you oppose him, or seek to wrench him from
his holdings. His stormy outbursts always leave

the moral atmosphere clear and bracing; he does not communicate the gloom and despondency he feels, because he brings us so directly and unfailingly in contact with the perennial sources of hope and faith, with the life-giving and the life-renewing. Though the heavens fall, the orbs of truth and justice fall not. Carlyle was like an unhoused soul, naked and bare to every wind that blows. He felt the awful cosmic chill. He could not take shelter in the creed of his fathers, nor in any of the opinions and beliefs of his time. He could not and did not try to fend himself against the keen edge of the terrible doubts, the awful mysteries, the abysmal questions and duties. He lived and wrought on in the visible presence of God. This was no myth to him, but a terrible reality. How the immensities open and yawn about him! He was like a man who should suddenly see his relations to the universe, both physical and moral, in gigantic perspective, and never through life lose the awe, the wonder, the fear, the revelation inspired. The veil, the illusion of the familiar, the commonplace, is torn away. The natural becomes the supernatural. Every question, every character, every duty, was seen against the immensities, like figures in the night against a background of fire, and seen as if for the first time. The sidereal, the cosmical, the eternal, — we grow familiar with these or lose sight of them entirely. But Carlyle never lost sight of them; his sense of them became morbidly acute, preternaturally developed, and it was as if

he saw every movement of the hand, every fall of
a leaf, as an emanation of solar energy.   A "haggard mood of the imagination" (his own phrase)
was habitual with him.   He could see only the
tragical in life and in history.   Events were immi-
nent, poised like avalanches that a word might
loosen.   We see Jeffries perpetually amazed at his
earnestness, the gradations in his mind were so
steep; the descent from the thought to the deed
was so swift and inevitable that the witty advocate
came to look upon him as a man to be avoided.

"Daily and hourly," he says (at the age of thirty-
eight), "the world natural grows more of a world
magical to me; this is as it should be.   Daily, too,
I see that there is no true poetry but in *reality*."

"The gist of my whole way of thought," he says
again, "is to raise the natural to the supernatural."
To his brother John he wrote in 1832: "I get
more earnest, graver, not unhappier, every day.
The whole creation seems more and more divine to
me, the natural more and more supernatural."   His
eighty-five years did not tame him at all, did not
blunt his conception of the "fearfulness and won-
derfulness of life."   Sometimes an opiate or an
anæsthetic operates inversely upon a constitution,
and, instead of inducing somnolence, makes the person wildly wakeful and sensitive.   The anodyne of
life acted this way upon Carlyle, and, instead of
quieting or benumbing him, filled him with portent-
ous imaginings and fresh cause for wonder.   There
is a danger that such a mind, if it takes to litera-

ture, will make a mess of it. But Carlyle is saved by his tremendous gripe upon reality. Do I say the ideal and the real were one with him? He made the ideal *the* real, and the only real. Whatever he touched he made tangible, actual, and vivid. Ideas are hurled like rocks, a word blisters like a branding-iron, a metaphor transfixes like a javelin. There is something in his sentences that lays hold of things, as the acids bite metals. His subtle thoughts, his marvelous wit, like the viewless gases of the chemist, combine with a force that startles the reader.

Carlyle differs from the ordinary religious enthusiast in the way he bares his bosom to the storm. His attitude is rather one of gladiatorial resignation than supplication. He makes peace with nothing, takes refuge in nothing. He flouts at happiness, at repose, at joy. "There is in man a *higher* than love of happiness; he can do without happiness, and instead thereof find blessedness." "The life of all gods figures itself to us as a sublime sadness, — earnestness of infinite battle against infinite labor. Our highest religion is named the ' Worship of Sorrow.' For the Son of Man there is no noble crown, well worn or even ill worn, but is a crown of thorns." His own worship is a kind of defiant admiration of Eternal Justice. He asks no quarter, and will give none. He turns upon the grim destinies a look as undismayed and as uncompromising as their own. Despair cannot crush him; he will crush it. The more it bears on, the harder he will work. The way to get rid of wretchedness is to despise it; the way to conquer the devil is to defy him; the way to gain heaven is to turn your back upon it, and be as unflinching as the gods themselves. Satan may be roasted in his own flames; Tophet may be exploded with its own sulphur. "Despicable biped!" (Teufelsdrökh is addressing himself.) "What is the sum total of the worst that lies before thee? Death? Well, death; and say the pangs of Tophet, too, and all that the devil and man may, will, or can do against thee! Hast thou not a heart? Canst thou not suffer what so it be, and as a child of freedom, though outcast, trample Tophet itself under thy feet while it consumes thee? Let it come, then; I will meet it and defy it." This is the "Everlasting No" of Teufelsdrökh, the annihilation of self. Having thus routed Satan with his own weapons, the "Everlasting Yea" is to people his domain with fairer forms; to find your ideal in the world about you. "Thy condition is but the stuff thou art to shape that same ideal out of; what matters whether such stuff be of this sort or of that, so the form thou give it be heroic, be poetic?" Carlyle's watchword through life, as I have said, was the German word *Entsagen*, or renunciation. The perfect flower of religion opens in the soul only when all self-seeking is abandoned. The divine, the heroic attitude is: "I ask not Heaven, I fear not Hell; I crave the truth alone, withersoever it may lead" "Truth! I cried, though the heavens

crush me for following her; no falsehood, though
a celestial lubberland were the price of apostasy."
The truth, — what is the truth? Carlyle answers:
That which you believe with all your soul and all
your might and all your strength, and are ready to
face Tophet for, — that, for you, is the truth.
Such a seeker was he himself. It matters little
whether we agree that he found it or not. The
law of this universe is such that where the love,
the desire, is perfect and supreme, the truth is
already found. That is the truth, not the letter
but the spirit; the seeker and the sought are one.
Can you by searching find out God? "Moses cried,
'When, O Lord, shall I find thee? God said,
Know that when thou hast sought thou hast already
found me.'" This is Carlyle's position, so far as
it can be defined. He hated dogma as he hated
poison. No direct or dogmatic statement of religious belief or opinion could he tolerate. He abandoned the church, for which his father designed
him, because of his inexorable artistic sense; he
could not endure the dogma that the church rested
upon, the pedestal of clay upon which the golden
image was reared. The gold he held to, as do all
serious souls, but the dogma of clay he quickly
dropped. "Whatever becomes of us," he said,
referring to this subject in a letter to a friend when
he was in his twenty-third year, "never let us
cease to behave like honest men."

IV

Carlyle had an enormous egoism, but to do the work he felt called on to do, to offset and withstand the huge, roaring, on-rushing modern world as he did, required an enormous egoism. In more senses than one do the words applied to the old prophet apply to him: "For, behold, I have made thee this day a defenced city, and an iron pillar, and brazen walls against the whole land, against the kings of Judah, against the princes thereof, against the priests thereof, and against the people of the land." He was a defenced city, an iron pillar, and brazen wall, in the extent to which he was riveted and clinched in his own purpose and aim, as well as in his attitude of opposition or hostility to the times in which he lived.

Froude, whose life of Carlyle in its just completed form, let me say here, has no equal in interest or literary value among biographies since his master's life of Sterling, presents his hero to us a prophet in the literal and utilitarian sense, as a foreteller of the course of events, and says that an adequate estimate of his work is not yet possible. We must wait and see if he was right about democracy, about America, universal suffrage, progress of the species, etc. "Whether his message was a true message remains to be seen." "If he was wrong he has misused his powers. The principles of his teaching are false. He has offered himself as a guide upon a road of which he had no know ledge; and his own desire for himself would be the speediest oblivion both of his person and his works."

But the man was true; there can be no doubt about that, and when such is the case the message may safely be left to take care of itself. We have got the full force and benefit of it in our own day and generation, whether our "cherished ideas of political liberty, with their kindred corollaries," prove illusions or not. All high spiritual and prophetic utterances are instantly their own proof and justification, or they are naught. Does Mr. Froude really mean that the prophecies of Jeremiah and Isaiah have become a part of the permanent "spiritual inheritance of mankind" because they were literally fulfilled in specific instances, and not because they were true from the first and always, as the impassioned yearnings and uprisings and reachings-forth of high God-burdened souls at all times are true? Regarded merely as a disturbing and overturning force, Carlyle was of great value. There never was a time, especially in an era like ours, when the opinion and moral conviction of the race did not need subsoiling, loosening up from the bottom, — the shock of rude, scornful, merciless power. There are ten thousand agencies and instrumentalities titillating the surface, smoothing, pulverizing, and vulgarizing the top. Chief of these is the gigantic, ubiquitous newspaper press, without character and without conscience; then the lyceum, the pulpit, the novel, the club, — all *cultivating* the superficies, and helping make life shallow and monotonous. How deep does the leading editorial go, or the review article, or the Sunday sermon? But such a force as Carlyle disturbs our complacency. Opinion is shocked, but it is deepened. The moral and intellectual resources of all men have been added to. But the literal fulfillment and verification of his prophecies, — shall we insist upon that? Is not a prophet his own proof, the same as a poet? Must we summon witnesses and go into the justice-court of fact? The only questions to be asked are: Was he an inspired man? was his an authoritative voice? did he touch bottom? was he sincere? was he grounded and rooted in character? It is not the stamp on the coin that gives it its value, though on the bank-note it is. Carlyle's words were not promises, but performances; they are good now if ever. To test him by his political opinions is like testing Shakespeare by his fidelity to historical fact in his plays, or judging Lucretius by his philosophy, or Milton or Dante by their theology. Carlyle was just as distinctively an imaginative writer as were any of these men, and his case is to be tried on the same grounds. It is his utterances as a seer touching conduct, touching duty, touching nature, touching the soul, touching life, that most concern us, — the ideal to be cherished, the standard he held to.

Carlyle was a poet touched with religious wrath and fervor, and he confronted his times and country as squarely and in the same spirit as did the old prophets. He predicts nothing, foretells nothing, except death and destruction to those who depart from the ways of the Lord, or, in modern phrase, from nature and truth. He shared the Hebraic sense of the awful mystery and fearfulness of life and the splendor and inexorableness of the moral law. His habitual mood was not one of contemplation and enjoyment, but of struggle and "desperate hope." The deep biblical word fear, — fear of the Lord, — he knew what that meant, as few moderns did.

He was antagonistic to his country and his times, and who would have had him otherwise? Let him be the hammer on the other side that clinches the nail. He did not believe in democracy, in popular sovereignty, in the progress of the species, in the political equality of Jesus and Judas; in fact, he repudiated with mingled wrath and sorrow the whole American idea and theory of politics: yet who shall say that his central doctrine of the survival of the fittest, the nobility of labor, the exaltation of justice, valor, pity, the leadership of character, truth, nobility, wisdom, etc., is really and finally inconsistent with, or inimical to, that which is valuable and permanent and formative in the modern movement? I think it is the best medicine and regimen for it that could be suggested, — the best stay and counterweight. For the making of good democrats, there are no books like Carlyle's, and we in America need especially to cherish him, and to lay his lesson to heart.

It is his supreme merit that he spoke with absolute sincerity; not according to the beliefs, traditions, conventionalities of his times, for they were mostly against him, but according to his private and solemn conviction of what the will of his Maker with reference to himself was. The reason why so much writing and preaching sounds hollow and insincere compared with his is that the writers and speakers are mostly under the influence of current beliefs or received traditions; they deliver themselves of what they have been taught, or what is fashionable and pleasant; they draw upon a sort of public fund of conviction and sentiment and not at all from original private resources, as he did. It is not their own minds or their own experience they speak from, but a vague, featureless, general mind and general experience. We drink from a cistern or reservoir and not from a fountain-head. Carlyle always takes us to the source of intense personal and original conviction. The spring may be a hot spring, or a sulphur spring, or a spouting spring, — a geyser, as Froude says, shooting up volumes of steam and stone, — or the most refreshing and delicious of fountains (and he seems to have been all these things alternately); but in any case it was an original source and came from out the depths, at times from out the Plutonic depths.

He bewails his gloom and loneliness, and the isolation of his soul in the paths in which he was called to walk. In many ways he was an exile, a wanderer, forlorn or uncertain, like one who had

missed the road, — at times groping about sorrow-
fully, anon desperately hewing his way through
all manner of obstructions. He presents the singular anomaly of a great man, of a towering and
unique genius, such as appears at intervals of centuries, who was not in any sense representative,
who had no precursors and who left no followers, —
a man isolated, exceptional, towering like a solitary
peak or cone set over against the main ranges. He
is in line with none of the great men, or small
men, of his age and country. His message is unwel-
come to them. He is an enormous reaction or
rebound from the all-leveling tendencies of democracy. No wonder he thought himself the most
solitary man in the world, and bewailed his loneliness continually. He was the most solitary. Of
all the great men his race and country have produced, none, perhaps, were quite so isolated and
set apart as he. None shared so little the life and
aspirations of their countrymen, or were so little
sustained by the spirit of their age. The literature,
the religion, the science, the politics of his times
were alike hateful to him. His spirit was as lonely
as a "peak in Darien." He felt himself on a narrow isthmus of time, confronted by two eternities,
— the eternity past and the eternity to come.
Daily and hourly he felt the abysmal solitude that
surrounded him. Endowed with the richest fund
of sympathy, and yet sympathizing with so little;
burdened with solicitude for the public weal, and
yet in no vital or intimate relation with the public

he would serve; deeply absorbed in the social and
political problems of his time, and yet able to arrive
at no adequate practical solution of them; passion-
ately relig·ous, and yet repudiating all creeds and
forms of worship; despising the old faiths, and dis-
gusted with the new; honoring science, and acknow-
ledging his debt to it, yet drawing back with horror
from conclusions to which science seemed inevit-
ably to lead; essentially a man of action, of deeds,
of heroic fibre, yet forced to become a "writer of
books;" a democrat who denounced democracy; a
radical who despised radicalism; "a Puritan without a creed."

These things measure the depth of his sincerity;
he never lost heart or hope, though heart and hope
had so little that was tangible to go upon.   He had
the piety and zeal of a religious devotee, without
the devotee's comforting belief; the fiery earnestness of a reformer, without the reformer's definite
aims; the spirit of science, without the scientific
coolness and disinterestedness; the heart of a hero,
without the hero's insensibilities; he had strugglings, wrestlings, agonizings, without any sense of
victory; his foes were invisible and largely imaginary, but all the more terrible and unconquerable
on that account.   Verily was he lonely, heavy
laden, and at best full of "desperate hope."   His
own work, which was accomplished with such pains
and labor throes, gave him no satisfaction.   When
he was idle, his demon tormented him with the
cry, "Work, work;" and when he was toiling at

his tasks, his obstructions, torpidities, and dispirit-
ments nearly crushed him.

It is probably true that he thought he had some
special mission to mankind, something as definite
and tangible as Luther had. His stress and heat
of conviction were such as only the great world-
reformers have been possessed of. He was burdened with the sins and follies of mankind, and
must mend them. His mission was to mend them,
but perhaps in quite other ways than he thought.
He sought to restore an age fast passing, — the age
of authority, the age of the heroic leader; but
toward the restoration of such age he had no effect
whatever. The tide of democracy sweeps on. He
was like Xerxes whipping the sea. His real mission he was far less conscious of, for it was what
his search for the hero implied and brought forward
that he finally bequeathed us. If he did not make
us long for the strong man to rule over us, he made
us love all manly and heroic qualities afresh, and as
if by a new revelation of their value. He made all
shallownesses and shams wear such a face as they
never before wore. He made it easier for all men
to be more truthful and earnest. Hence his final
effect and value was as a fountain of fresh moral
conviction and power. The old stock truths perpetually need restating and reapplying on fresh
grounds and in large and unexpected ways. And
how he restated them and reinforced them! veracity, sincerity, courage, justice, manliness, religious-
ness, — fairly burning them into the conscience of

his times. He took the great facts of existence out
of the mouths of priests, out of their conventional
theological swathing, where they were fast becoming mummified, and presented them *quick* or as
living and breathing realities.

It may be added that Carlyle was one of those
men whom the world can neither make nor break,
— a meteoric rock from out the fiery heavens,
bound to hit hard if not self-consumed, and not
looking at all for a convenient or a soft place to
alight, — a blazing star in his literary expression,
but in his character and purpose the most tangible
and unconquerable of men. "Thou, O World,
how wilt thou secure thyself against this man?
Thou canst not hire him by thy guineas, nor by
thy gibbets and law penalties restrain him. He
eludes thee like a Spirit. Thou canst not forward
him, thou canst not hinder him. Thy penalties,
thy poverties, neglects, contumelies: behold, all
these are good for him."

XI

AT SEA

ONE does not seem really to have got out-of-doors till he goes to sea. On the land he is shut in by the hills, or the forests, or more or less housed by the sharp lines of his horizon. But at sea he finds the roof taken off, the walls taken down; he is no longer in the hollow of the earth's hand, but upon its naked back, with nothing between him and the immensities. He is in the great cosmic out-of-doors, as much so as if voyaging to the moon or to Mars. An astronomic solitude and vacuity surround him; his only guides and landmarks are stellar; the earth has disappeared; the horizon has gone; he has only the sky and its orbs left; this cold, vitreous, blue - black liquid through which the ship plows is not water, but some denser form of the cosmic ether. He can now see the curve of the sphere which the hills hid from him; he can study astronomy under improved conditions. If he was being borne through the interplanetary spaces on an immense shield, his impressions would not perhaps be much different. He would find the same vacuity, the same blank or negative space, the same empty, indefinite, oppressive out-of-doors

For it must be admitted that a voyage at sea is more impressive to the imagination than to the actual sense. The world is left behind; all standards of size, of magnitude, of distance, are vanished; there is no size, no form, no perspective; the universe has dwindled to a little circle of crumpled water, that journeys with you day after day, and to which you seem bound by some enchantment. The sky becomes a shallow, close-fitting dome, or else a pall of cloud that seems ready to descend upon you. You cannot see or realize the vast and vacant surrounding; there is nothing to define it or set it off. Three thousand miles of ocean space are less impressive than three miles bounded by rugged mountains walls. Indeed, the grandeur of form, of magnitude, of distance, of proportion, are only upon shore. A voyage across the Atlantic is an eight or ten day sail through vacancy. There is no sensible progress; you pass no fixed points. Is it the steamer that is moving, or is it the sea? or is it all a dance and illusion of the troubled brain? Yesterday, to-day, and to-morrow, you are in the same parenthesis of nowhere. The three hundred or more miles the ship daily makes is ideal, not real. Every night the stars dance and reel there in the same place amid the rigging; every morning the sun comes up from behind the same wave, and staggers slowly across the sinister sky. The eye becomes a-hunger for form, for permanent lines, for a horizon wall to lift up and keep off the sky, and give it a sense of room. One understands why sailors become an imaginative and superstitious race; it is the reaction from this narrow horizon in which they are pent, — this ring of fate surrounds and oppresses them. They escape by invoking the aid of the supernatural. In the sea itself there is far less to stimulate the imagination than in the varied forms and colors of the land. How cold, how merciless, how elemental it looks!

The only things that look familiar at sea are the clouds. These are messengers from home, and how weary and disconsolate they appear, stretching out along the horizon, as if looking for a hill or mountain-top to rest upon, — nothing to hold them up, — a roof without walls, a span without piers. One gets the impression that they are grown faint, and must presently, if they reach much farther, fall into the sea. But when the rain came, it seemed like mockery or irony on the part of the clouds. Did one vaguely believe, then, that the clouds would respect the sea, and withhold their needless rain? No, they treated it as if it were a mill-pond, or a spring-run, too insignificant to make any exceptions to.

One bright Sunday, when the surface of the sea was like glass, a long chain of cloud-mountains lay to the south of us all day, while the rest of the sky was clear. How they glowed in the strong sunlight, their summits shining like a bouquet of full moons, and making a broad, white, or golden path upon the water! They came out of the southwest, an endless procession of them, and tapered away in

the east. They were the piled, convoluted, indo-
lent clouds of midsummer, — thunder-clouds that
had retired from business; the captains of the
storm in easy undress. All day they filed along
there, keeping the ship company. How the eye
reveled in their definite, yet ever-changing, forms!
Their under or base line was as straight and continuous as the rim of the ocean. The substratum of
air upon which they rested was like a uniform layer
of granite rock, invisible, but all-resisting; not one
particle of these vast cloud-mountains, so broken
and irregular in their summits, sank below this
aerial granite boundary. The equilibrium of the
air is frequently such that the under-surface of the
clouds is like a ceiling. It is a fair-weather sign,
whether upon the sea or upon the land. One may
frequently see it in a mountainous district, when
the fog-clouds settle down, and blot out all the tops
of the mountains without one fleck of vapor going
below a given line which runs above every valley,
as uniform as the sea-level. It is probable that in
fair weather the atmosphere always lies in regular
strata in this way, and that it is the displacement
and mixing up of these by some unknown cause
that produces storms.

As the sun neared the horizon these cloud-masses
threw great blue shadows athwart each other, which
afforded the eye a new pleasure.

Late one afternoon the clouds assumed a still
more friendly and welcome shape. A long, purple,
irregular range of them rose up from the horizon in

the northwest, exactly simulating distant mountains. The sun sank behind them, and threw out
great spokes of light as from behind my native Catskills. Then gradually a low, wooded shore came
into view along their base. It proved to be a fog-
bank lying low upon the water, but it copied exactly,
in its forms and outlines, a flat, umbrageous coast.
You could see distinctly where it ended, and where
the water began. I sat long on that side of the
ship, and let my willing eyes deceive themselves.
I could not divest myself of the comfortable feeling
inspired by the prospect. It was to the outward
sense what dreams and reveries are to the inward.
That blind, instinctive love of the land, — I did
not know how masterful and involuntary the impulse was, till I found myself warming up toward
that phantom coast. The empty void of the sea
was partly filled, if only with a shadow. The
inhuman desolation of the ocean was blotted out
for a moment, in that direction at least. What
phantom-huggers we are upon sea or upon land!
It made no difference that I knew this to be a sham
coast. I could feel its friendly influence all the
same, even when my back was turned.

In summer, fog seems to lie upon the Atlantic
in great shallow fleeces, looking, I dare say, like
spots of mould or mildew from an elevation of a
few miles. These fog-banks are produced by the
deep cold currents rising to the surface, and coming
in contact with the warmer air. One may see them
far in advance, looking so shallow that it seems as

if the great steamer must carry her head above
them.   But she does not quite do it.   When she
enters this obscurity, there begins the hoarse bellow-
ing of her great whistle.   As one dozes in his berth
or sits in the cabin reading, there comes a vague
impression that we are entering some port or harbor, the sound is so welcome, and is so suggestive
of the proximity of other vessels.   But only once
did our loud and repeated hallooing awaken any
response.   Everybody heard the answering whistle
out of the thick obscurity ahead, and was on the
alert.   Our steamer instantly slowed her engines
and redoubled her tootings.   The two vessels soon
got the bearing of each other, and the stranger
passed us on the starboard side, the hoarse voice of
her whistle alone revealing her course to us.

Late one afternoon, as we neared the Banks, the
word spread on deck that the knobs and pinnacles
of a thunder-cloud sunk below the horizon, and
that deeply and sharply notched the western rim of
the sea, were icebergs.   The captain was quoted as
authority.   He probably encouraged the delusion.
The jaded passengers wanted a new sensation.
Everybody was willing, even anxious, to believe
them icebergs, and some persons would have them
so, and listened coldly and reluctantly to any proof
to the contrary.   What we want to believe, what
it suits our convenience, or pleasure, or prejudice,
to believe, one need not go to sea to learn what
slender logic will incline us to believe.   To a firm,
steady gaze, these icebergs were seen to be momently

changing their forms, new chasms opening, new
pinnacles rising: but these appearances were easily
accounted for by the credulous; the ice mountains
were rolling over, or splitting asunder.   One of the
rarest things in the average cultivated man or
woman is the capacity to receive and weigh evidence
touching any natural phenomenon, especially at sea.
If the captain had deliberately said that the shift-
ing forms there on the horizon were only a school
of whales playing at leap-frog, all the women and
half the men among the passengers would have
believed him.

In going to England in early May, we encountered the fine weather, the warmth and the sunshine as of June, that had been "central" over the
British Islands for a week or more, five or six
hundred miles from shore.   We had come up from
lower latitudes, and it was as if we had ascended
a hill and found summer at the top, while a cold,
backward spring yet lingered in the valley.   But
on our return in early August, the positions of
spring and summer were reversed.   Scotland was
cold and rainy, and for several days at sea you
could in the distance hardly tell the sea from the
sky, all was so gray and misty.   In mid-Atlantic
we ran into the American climate.   The great continent, basking there in the western sun, and glowing with midsummer heat, made itself felt to the
centre of this briny void.   The sea detached itself
sharply from the sky, and became like a shield of
burnished steel, which the sky surrounded like a

dome of glass.   For four successive nights the sun
sank clear in the wave, sometimes seeming to melt
and mingle with the ocean.   One night a bank of
mist seemed to impede his setting.   He lingered a
long while partly buried in it, then slowly disappeared as through a slit in the vapor, which glowed
red-hot, a mere line of fire, for some moments
afterward.

As we neared home the heat became severe.
We were going down the hill into a fiery valley.
Vast stretches of the sea were like glass bending
above the long, slow heaving of the primal ocean.
Swordfish lay basking here and there on the sur-
face, too lazy to get out of the way of the ship: —

> "The air was calm, and on the level brine
> Sleek Panope with all her sisters played."

Occasionally a whale would blow, or show his glis-
tening back, attracting a crowd to the railing.   One
morning a whale plunged spitefully through the
track of the ship but a few hundred yards away.

But the prettiest sight in the way of animated
nature was the shoals of dolphins occasionally seen
during these brilliant torrid days, leaping and sporting, and apparently racing with the vessel.   They
would leap in pairs from the glassy surface of one
swell of the steamer across the polished chasm into
the next swell, frisking their tails and doing their
best not to be beaten.   They were like fawns or
young kine sporting in a summer meadow.   It was
the only touch of mirth, or youth and jollity, I saw
in the grim sea.   Savagery and desolation make up

the prevailing expression here. The sea-fowls have weird and disconsolate cries, and appear doomed to perpetual solitude. But these dolphins know what companionship is, and are in their own demesne. When one sees them bursting out of the waves, the impression is that school is just out; there come the boys, skipping and laughing, and, seeing us just passing, cry to one another: "Now for a race! Hurrah, boys! We can beat 'em!"

One notices any change in the course of the ship by the stars at night. For nearly a week Venus sank nightly into the sea far to the north of us. Our course coming home is south-southwest. Then, one night, as you promenade the deck, you see, with a keen pleasure, Venus through the rigging dead ahead. The good ship has turned the corner; she has scented New York harbor, and is making straight for it, with New England far away there on her right. Now sails and smoke-funnels begin to appear. All ocean paths converge here: full-rigged ships, piled with canvas, are passed, rocking idly upon the polished surface; sails are seen just dropping below the horizon, phantom ships without hulls, while here and there the black smoke of some steamer tarnishes the sky. Now we pass steamers that left New York but yesterday; the City of Rome — looking, with her three smoke-stacks and her long hull, like two steamers together — creeps along the southern horizon, just ready to vanish behind it. Now she stands in the reflected light of a great white cloud which makes a bright track

upon the water like the full moon.   Then she
slides on into the dim and even dimmer distance,
and we slide on over the tropic sea, and, by a splendid run, just catch the tide at the moment of its
full, early the next morning, and pass the bar off
Sandy Hook without a moment of time or an inch
of water to spare.

INDEX

Printed in the United Kingdom
by Lightning Source UK Ltd.
119681UK00001B/10